Trumpet
in Zion

Trumpet in Zion

Worship Resources, Year C

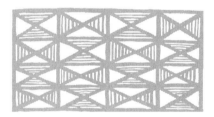

LINDA H. HOLLIES

THE PILGRIM PRESS   CLEVELAND

Dedication

This work is dedicated to my foremothers:

DORETHA ROBINSON ADAMS

LUCINDA ROBINSON WESTON

EUNICE ROBINSON WADE

LULA SMITH

LOUISE HOLLOWAY

DELLA BURT

HORTENSE HOUSE

REV. DR. JANET HOPKINS

The Pilgrim Press, 700 Prospect Avenue, Cleveland, Ohio 44115-1100
pilgrimpress.com
© 2003 by Linda H. Hollies

All rights reserved. Published 2003

Printed in the United States of America on acid-free paper

08   07   06   05   04   03   5   4   3   2   1

Library of Congress Cataloging-in-Publication Data

Hollies, Linda H.
    Trumpet in Zion : worship resources / Linda H. Hollies.
        p.   cm.
    Includes bibliographical references.
    Contents: [1] Year C.
    ISBN 0-8298-1558-9 (alk. paper)
    1. African American public worship.—2. Worship programs.—I. Title.

    BR563.N4 H653—2001
    264'.0089'96073—dc21

                                                    2001024585

CONTENTS

PROLOGUE

Theological reflection on the Scriptures is the work of the people. African American Christians have a deeply rooted tradition of learning, interpreting, reframing, and retelling the biblical story in light of their experiences. We are the people of God who grapple with the meaning of the Scriptures for our daily lives. We recognize that we are created in the image of God, with intelligence, creative powers, and abilities. We have also been mandated by God to give birth to new images, new beings, and new things. For we are a part of God's continuing creation story.

Trumpet in Zion is a new creation that seeks to address God in the voice, verbiage, and expression of African Americans at worship. Being a product of the Church of God, it has been my joy to wrestle with the lectionary passages and discover the shaded nuances, overt distinctions, and direct linkages to myself, my people, and our journey with God. As a pastor-teacher and faithful student of the living Word, I have delighted in looking at the old, old story through my Africentric, womanist eyes. My picture of and reflection on both God and the Scriptures has changed, grown, enlarged, and encompassed more images over the years, due to my education and experiences in the world.

This work is a new resource with a call to worship, call to confession, prayer of confession, words of assurance, responsive reading based on the Psalter, offertory invitation and praise, benediction, and blessing for each Sunday. (Scriptures are taken from the *Revised Common Lectionary, Year C.*) There are points where information is offered for the decoration of the altar around certain themes.

Trumpet in Zion is a "read-to-use" handbook for pastors and worship teams. It is an educational tool, offered to Christian educators for use in church school, confirmation, and small group study. It may be adapted for use by hospital and campus ministers in their settings. And *Trumpet in Zion* is a devotional guide for those who use the lectionary in a systematic fashion. Although the work is set for use with the lectionary, Year C, the materials may be used freely by those who do not follow the lectionary. All parts of the work are compatible for inspiring and promoting personal thoughts to flow from users.

My joy and delight has been the rewriting of the Psalter for use in the African American community. During an Annual Conference Spiritual Formation retreat, we focused on the Psalms, with Dr. Sister Nancy Shrank, author of *Psalms Anew.* Her teaching on the laments of David's community resounded in my spirit. As an assignment was given to rewrite a psalm for my life, this work was born. *Trumpet in Zion* is my response to God's call to "Cry loud, spare not, lift up your voice, like a trumpet in Zion. Show my people their transgressions, and the house of Jacob their sin." (Isaiah 58:1) These are written as responsive readings to be both the celebrations and laments of worshiping communities.

I am well aware that the limits of this work are due to the boundaries of my worldview, education, and life experiences. However, I offer this volume in memory of the ancestors who spoke to God in their own unique, broken, and colorful language; I offer it in celebration of the churches that I have pastored. These faithful souls have allowed me to "practice" liturgies with them each Sunday and on special occasions. I offer it in hope, for the generations that are to follow. They need a record of our praying for them. They need a chronicle of our journey with God.

Rev. Dr. Linda H. Hollies
Grand Rapids, Michigan

PREFACE

Liturgy is the work of the people in the life of public worship. Liturgy encompasses the diverse ways that we rehearse our faith story when we gather as a worshiping community. Liturgy is one of the ways we attempt to give voice to our feeble and inarticulate praise of God. Therefore, liturgy must be inclusive. Liturgy must address the traditional manner of prayer. Liturgy must also speak in the common vernacular of the younger people. Liturgy must look backwards to take stock of our multiple histories, our compound cultures, both of Africa and upon the shores of this country. Liturgy must address our rich heritage of struggle, survival, accomplishments, and exploits. And liturgy must also speak to the realities of our current situations in the songs we sing, prayers we pray, and sermons we preach. Liturgy is not stagnant. It is a live, swiftly moving river that aims at keeping our inarticulate and spoken relationship with God fresh and ever flowing.

This work begins at the beginning of the liturgical year, with Advent season. Advent is that waiting period for the Christ to come afresh into our conscious awareness. It is also the season when we acknowledge the significant contributions of the Christ Child's mother, Mary, and his cousin, John, and John's mother, Elizabeth. For Advent serves as a reminder that for over four hundred years God had been silent in Israel. That blank page between the last chapter of Malachi and the first page of Matthew signifies the time of no new inspiration or revelation from God! God's first words after four hundred years come with the announcement of two boy children who will emerge from the wombs of their pregnant mothers. Advent is a season of waiting for birth. Advent is a season of getting ready, preparing and seeking a clean, accepting, and hospitable space for the birth.

I began this work while serving in the Land of Wait! This land is where you wait for the proper time to give birth. This is the time when the pregnancy has to bloom from gestation into an infant who will be born and thrive in today's world. This Land of Wait is an interesting place to be involved in as an author. For in this place one begins to devoutly seek fresh manna from the Living Word! One struggles, straining to hear a Word from the Lord on the real side! I questioned my faith in these scriptures that I have quoted, utilized, and written about in the past. Writing Year C of *Trumpet in Zion* finds me not as pastor of a primarily Anglo congregation, as when I wrote Year B. I write while sitting in a "strange land" of "foreign" people. As a United Methodist clergywoman, I have written before from a familiar context among Methodist, primarily Anglo, congregants. Of course, you are aware that our cultural context for ministry certainly impacts our thinking, pondering, planning, praying, and writing.

Let me explain how I arrived in the Land of Wait. The Anglo congregation I was pastor of while writing for Year B was very tentative about having a woman pastor for the first time in their history. They were especially concerned about having an African American woman who was bodacious! Perhaps had I been a bit more refined, laid back, and restrained in my verbiage and dress, they might have been more comfortable. However, I am who I am! And I was not a "fit" for them. They were not a "fit" for me. We did try it for a year. It was the year from hell!

The charge leveled against me was for "changing their congregation's face" as more people of color came to visit. I dared to challenge their "good works abroad," while they let me know, with clarity, that they were not the least bit interested in rehab of the blighted homes just three blocks "down the street"! They wanted me to preach "nice" sermons with a smile on my face as I stroked them for their history. Honestly, I tried. It simply wasn't me!

Let me tell you about my state of shock when I was forced to leave that church. Then, talk about pain. Talk about anger. Now, let's talk about major depression! Let's talk about wrestling with my faith in God. Let's talk about grappling with my call to ministry and the surrounding issues of my professional identity. And, certainly, let's talk about how the Scriptures seemed to mock me, make fun of me, and hurt me even more. For the "Word" that came to me was from Psalm 46:10: "Be still and know that I am God." Being still put me in the Land of Wait. Being still is an act of prayer!

September 11, 2001 found me and the nation needing to hear from God. My only two black neighbors belonged to the same congregation, New Hope Missionary Baptist Church. Both the Littles and the Cockrells invited us to visit with them. The pastor, Rev. Derrick Lewis-Noble, preached "God Has the Last Word!" Mista Chuck and I believed him. We have been attending faithfully with Giraurd.

Pastor Noble has allowed me the distinct opportunity to be the first woman ever to preach from the pulpit, to baptize believers into the faith, and to consecrate communion in the eighty-six-year history of this congregation! Pastor Noble has given me the privilege of having an office to do pastoral counseling in a Baptist Church where the needs are multiple and varied. And Pastor Noble welcomed me to New Hope at a time when I didn't have a "home." So, I have seen the Word through a different lens this past year. I sit on a "black Baptist" pulpit, often never saying an official word, but making a loud and clear statement by merely sitting there.

I'm needed where I am, as uncomfortable as it feels most days. For if I left, who would tell the story of Zion as viewed by a trained female? If I left, who would be the trumpet for those women who have sat, bound, in the pews for generations, hesitating to enter the "strange" but sacred space of professional ministry? This past March, for the first time in history, women joined the ranks of those serving communion at New Hope Missionary Baptist Church. A woman, Mrs. Endia Weekly, is chair of the trustee board at New Hope Missionary Baptist Church. And women are in training to become deacons and break up the "old boys club"!

While serving in the Land of Wait, a new ministry has been birthed through this broken vessel. WomanSpace: A Sacred Space for God's Bodacious Woman, now opened and thriving, is a gathering place, a counseling center, a networking spot for "going-somewhere women" who have decided to tap into their spiritual foundation through pastoral counseling and spiritual direction. I've discovered that the Land of Wait is a birthing center!

Therefore, I continue to write. And I wait, not in anxious hope, but in expectation. For I know that a new story always emerges when we pray. For liturgy is actually a form of serious prayer. *Trumpet in Zion,* Year C, simply calls out the news of what happens when the people of God pray, in faith, believing that God does yet hear us and will answer our petitions!

Prayer is a corporate experience in these liturgies. For worship is the work of the whole Body. Prayer is the hopes, the fears, the anxieties, and the faith of a collective group of pilgrims on a journey. In our silence, we pray. In our singing, we pray. Often, in our reading of the Word, we are at prayer, especially as we read the Psalms. Only God can articulate the many facets of prayer as we approach the altar in churches across the world, with our needs accompanying us to worship. So the officers of our local congregations pray for us. The choirs and soloists pray for us. The leader of corporate prayer takes our petitions before God's throne. Thank God that often there is a pastoral prayer as someone gives voice to the concerns that leave us speechless. The good news most days is that even our sighs, our groans, and our tears are prayers. For our God translates them as prayers.

Writing can be a solitary event. Yet, there are individuals in my life whom I cannot do without. The list is headed by my husband, Charles H. Hollies, who takes better care of me than I often deserve. My grandson, Giraud Chase Hollies, is the joy of my life and my inspiration for the days to come. My children are my motivation for leaving what I have learned documented on paper. Gregory Raymond, Grelon Renard, Grian Eunyke and her children Germal Chasad and Symphony will allow me to live in the coming generations. My siblings push, promote, and support me; they are the essence of "family" at its best: sisters Jacqui Brodie-Davis and Bob; Riene Morris; Regina Pleasant and Arthur; and my brothers James Adams and Jeannette; Eddie Adams and Onnette; David Adams and Kim; and Robert Adams and Lisa.

I honor a group of sister-friends who nourish my soul: Barbara Jean Vinson; Rev. Vera Jo Edington; Alberta Petrosko; Rev. Daisy Thomas-Quinney; Rev. Dr. Eleanor Miller; Rev. Beverly Garvin; Rev. Louisa Martin; Rev. Harlene Harden; Rev. Joyce E. Wallace; Rev. Genevieve Brown; Rev. Michelle Cobb; Rev. Dr. Valerie Davis; Rev. Ida Easley; Rev. Carolyn Abrams; Rev. Dr. Linda Boston; Rev. Cynthia Stewart; Rev. Constance Wilkerson; Rev. Dr. Vanessa Stephens-Lee; Rev. Dr. Cynthia Belt; and Rev. Carolyn Wilkins. Each of these women counsels, prays with and for, challenges, and loves me so that writing flows, preaching continues, and my spirit is continually renewed. I count each one of these women as blessings, gifts, and treasures in my life.

Then there are my brother-friends and their spouses, whose love uplifts me and makes me more secure in my position in the family of God. Rev. Anthony and Rev. Bobbi Earl, Rev. Dr. Michael and Minister Katheryn Carson, Rev. Donald Guest, Rev. Dr. Zawdie Abiade, Rev. Bennie and First Lady Caroline Liggins, Rev. Richard and Carolyn Washington, and our adopted children, Rev. Dr. Dennis and Rev. Darlene Robinson, accept me fully as they uphold my life and ministry in their gentle hands. Without them, my life would be so incomplete. But, because of them, I am more wholly alive in the body of Christ.

Writing broadens my community. For now you have become a part of my world! I pray that this work will stimulate you to begin painting your own canvas with wide, happy, and life-changing strokes. One of my seminary professors and friend, Dr. Emma Justes, taught me that the Bible not only speaks to us, but speaks about us, individually! Every one of us can encounter our God and ourselves anew as we read and reflect upon the living Word.

Lastly, this book is dedicated to the enabling ministry of the Reverend Derrick Lewis-Noble. He was the baby of eight siblings. His mother died while he was very young and his father had to be institutionalized for health reasons. Derrick and two other siblings were reared by his oldest sister and her spouse. Vervel Nobel-Ewing and Rev. J. W. Ewing opened their hearts and their homes that, of course, included the local church.

Derrick Lewis-Noble is one of the names to be on the alert for in the years to come. The African American Pulpit Board of Directors has named him one of "The Top 20 Young (Great) Revivalists" to watch in this century! (*African American Pulpit,* winter issue, 2001–2002).

Mista Chuck, Giraurd, and I collectively bless him and pray God's best all the days of his life and effective ministry! It is with a big sista's pride that I dedicate this work, *Trumpet in Zion,* Year C, to him.

Let us continue to pray together as we worship God in spirit and in truth. To God be all the glory!

Shalom my friends, God's best shalom!
Sista Linda

1 · THE ADVENT SEASON

Advent means Mary is pregnant! A baby is on the way. It makes no difference whether you want a baby, like babies, have wished for one, or even hate the thought of noisy, intruding infants! A baby is coming! We are forced to get ready.

An announcement of pregnancy hits folks in different ways. Not everyone is happy. Some folks are content with the way things are and don't want their satisfaction disrupted with a new baby in the house. For a baby means that new arrangements have to be made. The baby must have some place decent to sleep. The baby must have something adequate to wear. The baby must have sufficient provisions made for its arrival. And the most important thing an unborn baby needs is good prenatal care.

Advent is our prenatal care period! For good prenatal exams and regular follow-ups usually mean that health care providers won't have to spend a lot of money in the future with a sickly child. Parents won't have to expend as much energy with an ill infant. It pays in many ways to adequately prepare for the birth of a baby while we await its arrival.

When God says "Live," babies live. We can try in all sorts of ways to kill new life. But Advent says that a new baby will be born. And, since Mary has already birthed Jesus into the earthly realm, this season is one that you and I need to understand as our pregnancies! Like Mary, we too are pregnant. Like Mary, we too need a new community. Like Mary, we too have to walk, talk, cry, and sing a new song. And, like Mary, we too must find companions along the way to encourage us while we wait together.

The angel comes to the priest who cannot receive the great promise. He is silenced during the wait. The angel goes to a virgin girl who says "Yes" to the great promise. She is silenced as she walks to the home of the priest and his pregnant wife. When the pregnant wife goes to greet the silent virgin, the Holy Spirit descends, and singing and dancing begin. Elizabeth is filled with the Holy Spirit. Mary sings Hannah's old song. John the Baptist dances in his mother's womb. And the world waits for the birth of a newborn King!

Mary signifies the Church of God, the Bride of Jesus Christ. And every bride is to have a baby or the bridegroom will be embarrassed. For a marriage is an indication that offspring will come forth if at all possible. So the Bridegroom is waiting to see just what new life we will bring forth in our local houses of worship. Mary was not ready for this unplanned pregnancy! She didn't dream of it, wish for it, plan for it, or ask for it. Yet she said "Yes!" to God's divine plan to birth Jesus. During this Advent season, so will we! Don't fear, when we say "Yes!" to carrying and birthing God's child, all the "child support" that we need will be forthcoming. For during the wait we will live, like Mary, by our faith in a faithful God.

Altar Focus

Build the altar each week, beginning with a scene that speaks to the congregation about waiting, watching, preparing, and hoping. Positioning a glass star to twinkle over an empty shelter could begin Week One. During Week Two, animals might be placed in strategic places. For Week Three, an empty manger can be brought center stage, along with different types of shepherds. During Week Four, the parental figures of Mary and Joseph can be seen. On Christmas Eve, an array of angels might be appropriate, along with many different types of candles representing the light that is to come. The infant figure does not appear until Christmas Day. I suggest you place a large loaf of brown bread in the manger. Jesus is the bread of life and was born to die. It is not appropriate for us simply to get misty-eyed over the babe in the manger without realizing the fullness of his Advent.

To include the congregation in building the altar and the spirit of anticipation, ask them to bring animals, shepherds, and angels from home. After lighting the Advent candle, these gifts can be brought forward.

Many churches place poinsettias around the altar for the Christmas Eve worship. They should not detract from the focus of the worship setting. Sufficient room always needs to be left for the sacrament to be placed. Beauty ought never compromise our true and authentic worship!

FIRST SUNDAY OF ADVENT

Jeremiah 33:14–16
Psalm 25:1–10
1 Thessalonians 3:9–13
Luke 21:25–36

Call to Worship

Leader: People of God, hold on!
People: The Promised One is on the way.
Leader: People of God, we are in the season of serious waiting. The time is right for clearing out the mangers of our hearts.
People: God's Word is sure. We wait in anticipation.
Leader: The Righteous Branch of David is our Savior.
People: Justice will reign and salvation will be exalted.
Leader: People of God, give out a shout!
People: The Holy One is coming soon! We wait for his Advent with worship and praise.

Lighting of Advent Candle

Today we begin another intentional period of active waiting for the Christ. In this season we will slow our pace, be more generous in our outlook, and discover the many ways we have denied Christ access to our hearts. This candle lighting is only a reminder that the season of waiting has begun. We are awaiting the God who always comes.

Call to Confession

There will be signs in the sun, the moon, and the stars, and on the earth distress among nations is confused by the roaring of the sea and the waves. People will faint from fear and foreboding of what is coming upon the world, for the powers of the heavens will be shaken. Then they will see the Son of God coming in a cloud with power and with glory. Our confession makes us ready to receive the Second Coming. Shall we pray?

Confession

God, you have called us to be on guard so that our hearts are not weighed down with dissipation, drunkenness, and the worries of life. Advent catches us unexpectedly and not prepared. We ask for forgiveness of our sin and strength to be alert at all times by the power of your Holy Spirit. We want to be ready when Jesus comes. We pray in his name.

Words of Assurance

Heaven and earth will pass away, but the Words of God are sure. In the name and power of Jesus Christ, we are forgiven. Thanks be unto God.

Responsive Reading

Leader: Hey, God, it's us again! We are waiting and seeking your divine intervention.

People: God, we trust you and you alone. Don't allow us to be put to shame as we wait now. We need you to show up and to show out now!

Leader: God of the ancients, let the wicked be shamed openly.

People: God, would you please do something about the treacherous and the evil all around us? We are engaged in war and their side seems to be winning. We are waiting on you!

Leader: Lion of the Tribe, please keep us in your righteous path. In our time of waiting fix our hearts to hold your Son with love.

People: Make our directions clear. Lead us, guide us, and we will follow willingly. We believe your reputation that you always show up on time.

Leader: Great God, we remember your history among our ancestors.

People: We are waiting and asking you for an encore performance.

Leader: Because you are the Sovereign, wipe out our sin. Cover us with your cleansing blood. Make us wholly pure.

People: We want to be living testimonies! Like the ancestors, we yearn to do your righteous will. Your steadfast love and unfailing faithfulness encourage us to hold onto your unchanging hand. We wait for only you.

Offertory Invitation

Paul asked the Church at Thessalonica, "How can we thank God enough?" The question is relative today. For God is faithful! Our sharing in giving to support the ministry of Jesus Christ is evidence of our faithfulness. We can't beat God's giving!

Offertory Praise

God, we pray most earnestly that we may see you face to face. May this offering be a symbol of how we are increasing and abounding in love for one another and for all, just as we abound in love for you. So strengthen our hearts in holy living that we may be blameless before you at the time of your coming. We pray so with all the saints in the name of the Soon Coming King.

Benediction

Leader: Go! Be the Living Word in a world awaiting the Christ.
People: We will pray most earnestly that we may see God face to face.
Leader: I pray that God restores whatever is lacking in our faith as we wait.
People: Now, may our God and Sovereign direct our ways this week.
Leader: And may the empowering grace of Jesus Christ and the glorious power of the Holy Spirit make us increase and abound in love for one another and for all the people of God, so that at the Advent we will be blameless in our hearts by our holy living. Go in grace and shalom!
People: And it is so! Glory, hallelujah!

SECOND SUNDAY OF ADVENT

Malachi 3:1–4
Luke 1:68–79
Philippians 1:3–11
Luke 3:1–6

Call to Worship

Leader: The Messenger will arrive soon!
People: We are waiting for his Advent!
Leader: Certainly, Jesus is coming. Worship serves to help prepare our hearts.
People: We gather to worship the Coming One in spirit and in truth.

Candle Lighting

We light this candle with anticipation. For the Messenger of the covenant has come and the world has known him. He promised never to leave us nor to forsake us. We serve the God who always shows up in order to show out. May this candle serve as our reminder that he is coming again and the Advent will be soon.

Call to Confession

Prepare the way of the Christ, called Isaiah. Make his paths straight. For every valley shall be exalted and every mountain and hill shall be brought down, the crooked shall be made straight, and the rough ways made smooth. All flesh shall see the salvation of God. Confession keeps us in shape to return with Christ when he comes. Let's pray.

Confession

God, who can endure the day of your coming? Who will be able to stand when you appear in the sky? For you will be like a refiner's fire and like fuller's soap. You will sit as a refiner and purifier of silver. And you will purify the saints of God like gold. We pray forgiveness for the sin within us. Make us ready to see you, face to face, we pray in the name of the One who came to come again.

Responsive Reading

Leader: God's favor continues to shine upon us.

People: God's amazing grace keeps us despite our sinful selves.

Leader: The first advent of Jesus secured for us a sanctuary in God.

People: The ancient ones kept telling the story of salvation. Now we know for ourselves.

Leader: We have learned how to be saved from every hateful enemy by turning to God.

People: Our abiding trust is in a merciful Savior who is a shelter in every storm of life.

Leader: Our sure confidence binds us to the everlasting covenant.

People: With the second advent we shall live in holiness and righteousness through eternity.

Leader: Because of God's tender mercy we are forgiven our sin and made right with God.

People: We praise God for the Light that guides us towards everlasting peace.

Offertory Invitation

I thank God for every offering time that arrives. For we are constantly praying that God will give us opportunities to share the good news. And, because we share in the spreading of God's Word, we are confident that the One who began a good work in us will bring it to completion by the day of Jesus Christ's appearing. Let us give with generous spirits.

Offertory Praise

Having produced the harvest of righteousness that comes through Jesus Christ for the glory and praise of God, we have given of our resources. It is our prayer, God, that you will honor our giving, so that your love will continue to overflow so that more people will come to knowledge of you through Jesus Christ, in whose name we pray. Amen.

Benediction

Leader: The Christ has gone before us to prepare the way. By the forgiveness of our sin, by the tender mercies of our God, and by the breathing of the Holy Spirit we can walk in the peaceful power of our salvation. May God grant us wisdom to take our light to those who don't know Christ. May we receive power to be bold enough to go to those in places of death and guide them into the holy way of shalom! Go, working out your own soul's salvation as we wait.

People: Jesus Christ is the way, the truth, and the light. We leave to proclaim his name. Amen.

THIRD SUNDAY OF ADVENT

Zephaniah 3:14–20
Isaiah 12:2–6
Philippians 4:4–7
Luke 3:7–18

Call to Worship

Leader: Sing aloud, people of Zion! Rejoice and exult with all your heart.
People: The Sovereign God has taken away every judgment against us and even turned away our enemies.
Leader: The King of Glory is in our midst. We don't have to fear disaster anymore. Put away fear, people of God. Experience the strength of God within.
People: God rejoices over us with gladness and renews us with refreshing love. We will show our thanks with worship in this house of praise.

Candle Lighting

We await the God who heals. The lame and the outcast will gather. The blind and the weak will have great joy at his Advent. We light this candle in expectation of the day of his appearing. For all of us who have clean hearts will have our fortunes restored and our spirits gladdened, and our eternal home will be with God. Thanks be to the God who comes again and again.

Call to Confession

Even now the ax is laid at the root of the trees and every tree that does not bear good fruit will be cut down and thrown into the fire when God comes again. We know what we must do to be ready when that great day comes. Let us offer our prayers of confession.

Confession

God, John called us vipers, snakes, and evildoers. And we know that we are! For no good thing dwells in us. This time of serious waiting has been difficult, for we want to do right, but wrong is so easily available. Take away our bent towards sin. Cleanse us. Forgive us, we pray.

Words of Assurance

The Sovereign God is in our midst, a warrior who gives us the victory over the power of canceled sin. This is good news. Thanks be unto God. We are forgiven.

Responsive Reading

Leader: Surely God is our sure salvation!
People: We will trust and not be afraid. God is our perfect strength and might.
Leader: In our waiting God has become our salvation.
People: With joy we can draw living water from the Wellspring of Life.
Leader: And we will say this day:
People: Thanks be unto our God. We will make known the great deeds of God on our behalf. We will proclaim to the whole world that the name of our God is exalted.

Offertory Invitation

The Word of God calls us to not extort money from anyone by threats or false accusation. We are to be satisfied with our blessings and show our thankfulness as we return thanksgiving in our offerings. God loves a cheerful giver. Let us share with generous joy.

Offertory Praise

God, your winnowing fork is in your hand. You will clear the threshing floor and gather wheat into your granary, and the chaff you will burn with unquenchable fire. We have given to add to your harvest. Bless us in the name of the One who gave us all, we pray. Amen.

Benediction

Leader: My sisters and brothers, go rejoicing in the One who is coming always. Again, I say rejoice. Let our gentleness be known to everyone as we wait. The Sovereign is near. Do not worry about anything, but in everything by prayer and supplication, with thanksgiving, let our requests be known to God. And the peace of God, which surpasses all understanding, will guard our hearts and our minds in Christ Jesus.
People: It is so!

FOURTH SUNDAY OF ADVENT

Micah 5:2–5a
Luke 1:47–55
Hebrews 10:5–10
Luke 1:39–55

Call to Worship

People: The Advent approaches. The King of Glory arrives soon.
Leader: Mary's labor will soon begin.
People: We gather as midwives to assist with the birth.
Leader: For a son will be given unto us. He will stand and feed his flock.
People: Majesty, honor, dominion, and power belong to Mary's Little Lamb. We have come to worship and to adore the Prince of Peace.

Candle Lighting

Today we light the candle of hope. Our hope is in the One who shall be great to the ends of the earth. May this candle symbolize all those who have their hope anchored in the Promised One. With this light, we now pray for peace in Jerusalem and the rest of God's beloved world.

Call to Confession

When Christ came into the world, he said, "Sacrifices and offerings God does not desire." What God requires is a pure heart that is ready to receive the gift of the Advent. Let us pray.

Confession

God, neither burnt offerings nor sin offerings satisfied your requirements for being in relationship with you. Thank you for sending the Only Begotten Son, who came as the perfect sacrifice and became our atonement. Forgive us the sin that separates us. For it's in Jesus' name that we pray.

Words of Assurance

Leader: Brothers and sisters, it is by the will of God that we have been sanctified through the offering of the body of Christ once and for all. This is our good news.
People: Thanks be unto God for the gift of salvation. Amen.

Responsive Reading

Leader: Let's join in singing the song of Mary's praise.

People: We are blessed to be a blessing to the world.

Leader: Why are we so favored that the Almighty would dare to dwell among us?

People: We are made a little lower than angels and given power to choose the Christ.

Leader: Every promise God has made belongs to all those who will accept the gift of Life.

People: We are bursting with the good news. Our feet want to dance. Our lips want to give great praise. God's love for us has been made tangible and lives in us.

Leader: What God has done cannot be forgotten. We have been set apart due to God's great love towards us.

People: The news will never get old. The story will continue to be told. God's mercies endure forever.

Offertory Invitation

God continues to look with favor on the lowliness of willing servants. Surely from now on, all generations will call us blessed. The Mighty God has done great things for us. Let us give generously.

Offertory Praise

God, you have shown strength, scattered the proud in the thoughts of their hearts, brought down the powerful, and lifted the lowly. By your great mercies you have been our help. Receive our meager tokens of gratitude, we pray in the name of Jesus Christ.

Benediction

Leader: Make haste to leave this sanctuary and tell the world that the wait is almost over! Go and tell the world that God has blessed you beyond measure. Go and share your joy in such a way that those who hear your greeting are blessed by your very presence. Go in faith, love, and power, the trifold blessings of God, Jesus Christ, and the Holy Spirit.

People: So it is!

CHRISTMAS EVE

Isaiah 9:2–7
Psalm 96
Titus 2:11–14
Luke 2:1–14

Call to Worship

Leader: On this night we join with Mary in bringing forth the new and the different into our world.

People: We are the midwives who will call out the right time to pant and to push.

Leader: Our hearts have been cleansed and our spirits made right to house the new baby.

People: The waiting is almost over. The angelic choir is ready to begin their songs. A live birth requires that we become risk takers, willing to accept the new baby into our midst. On this night we are ready.
O come, O come, Emmanuel.

Candle Lighting

Unto us a child has been born. Unto us a son has been given. Authority rests upon his shoulders. And he is called Wonderful Counselor, Mighty God, Everlasting God, Prince of Peace. His authority shall grow continually, and there shall be endless peace for the throne of David. He will establish and uphold God's realm with justice and with righteousness from this time forward and forever more. On this night we light the Christ Candle in honor of him who has come, is present, and will come again.

Responsive Reading

Leader: New music is demanded on this most holy night.

People: We want to sing the worthiness of the Ancient of Days.

Leader: Let us declare the glory of God. Let us celebrate with musical chords that excel over what has been heard before.

People: Handel did not say it all with the "Hallelujah Chorus."

Leader: Quincy Jones did not have the last word with "The Soulful Messiah."

People: There is more intensity, drama, and harmony that needs to call out what God has done.

Leader: Let us call for the best musicians. Allow the greatest singers to lift their gifts in praise.

People: None of the best that we have—Kirk, Yolanda, Smallwood, nor the Williams Brothers—can do justice to the music that we need to exalt the God who keeps coming to see about us.

Leader: On this night the cacophony of nature's sounds join the angels in lifting praise to the Ancient of Days.

People: Splendor, power, majesty, and exquisite symphonies cannot meter enough harmonies to contain the hallelujahs we owe God.

Leader: So we will simply offer God the melody of our lives.

People: The strings of our hearts sing out praise. Our voices are tuned with the perfect pitch of praise. And our knees bow in humble adoration before the Great I Am. The God who came will come again. This is our certain hope and our excellent hymn for God.

Offertory Invitation

For the grace of God has appeared, bringing salvation to all. We have been trained to renounce unholy living and worldly passions. We have been called to live lives that are self-controlled, upright, and godly while we wait for the blessed hope and the manifestation of the glory of our great God, Jesus Christ. He it is who gave himself for us that he might redeem us from all sin. We can do no less as we share in this offering on this special night.

Offertory Praise

God, you are sovereign and we worship you with our gifts. Tonight the heavens are glad, the sea roars, the earth exalts in your wonder. Please accept our song of joy that we share in these offerings in Jesus' name.

Benediction

Leader: Do not be afraid! For see, I am bringing you good news of great joy for all people. To you is born this day, in the city of David, a Savior, who is the Messiah, Christ the Lord. This will be a sign for you; you will find a child wrapped in bands of cloth and lying in a manger.

People: Glory to God in the highest heaven, and on earth let there be peace. Hallelujah!

2 · THE CHRISTMAS SEASON

The Hope of the world is Jesus! We celebrate his moving into our skin, sharing our humanity, and winning for us the victory over death, the grave, and hell. Christmas is not simply one day. Christmas is a season of sharing the mystery of God's love made manifest in Jesus Christ. Christmas is a season of wonder, where the Babe in Bethlehem captures the attention of the whole world. Christmas is the season of new hope, new joy, and a newfound sense of community. May this be a Mary's Christmas for you and your congregation! Look for the angels. Watch for the stars. Prepare for the shepherds. Be in tune with the angelic songs. Open your heart and allow there to be room in the inn of your heart!

Christmas is the season that leads us into Epiphany, where we are urged to be on the lookout for signs of Christ's presence in our midst.

CHRISTMAS DAY · PROPER 1

Isaiah 9:2–7
Psalm 96
Titus 2:11–14
Luke 2:1–20

Call to Worship

Leader: Arise! Shine! Let's give God glory and praise!
People: We who have walked in gloom have experienced a new light. Jesus Christ the Savior is born!
Leader: Yokes have been broken, the rod of the oppressor is smashed, and slavery is abolished forever!
People: A child has been born, a Son given unto us. Power and authority are invested in him.
Leader: His name is Wonderful Counselor, Mighty God, Everlasting Creator, and Prince of Peace.
People: This God of shalom is our God, and Zion will forever worship in spirit and in truth. Amen.

Lighting the Christ Candle

It's an awesome story, this birth of a babe in Bethlehem. It's been told over and over again. Homeless parents, with no family around, are forced to have their child in a stable, filled with animals and awful smells. The Child of Peace is laid in a manger, signifying that he is food for the hungry and bread in a starving land. This infant was born to die! The stars danced, the angels sang a cantata, and animals bowed low in humble submission, representing us before the lover of our souls. We light this candle today, because we were not there to participate in the birthday party of the Son of the Most High God. But when he comes again, we will be present!

Call to Confession

On this holy day, our hearts need to be the cradle of love, tenderly holding the Savior of the world. Let our confession prepare us for this awesome duty.

Silent Confession

Words of Assurance

For us, Mary had a little Lamb, and Jesus is his name! Thanks be unto God. Amen.

Responsive Reading

Leader: Let's sing unto the Lord a new song!
People: Our God is an awesome God!
Leader: Bless the Lord; tell of this great salvation from day to day.
People: What a mighty God we serve!
Leader: Declare the Sovereign's glory among the people.
People: Our God reigns!
Leader: Great is the Lord, greatly to be praised!
People: Go, tell it upon the mountain!
Leader: Honor and Majesty, Strength and Beauty are strong names of God in this sanctuary.
People: Come by here, Good Lord!
Leader: Give the Power that Saves, glory. Bring an appropriate offering of thanksgiving.
People: What shall I render?
Leader: Simply worship the Lord in the beauty of holiness. For our God reigns!
People: Ain't dat good news! Amen!

Offertory Invitation

The grace of God has appeared, bringing salvation to us all. While we have waited for this blessed hope, today is the manifestation of God's abundant and abounding love for us. While we were yet sinners, God loved us and sent Jesus to be born, just to die for us! God has already given unto us. Let us now respond to this glorious gift.

Offertory Praise

Glory to God in the highest and on earth, peace! Thank you, Amazing God, for giving us eternal life in Jesus Christ. May our offerings spread the compassion, the healing, and the work of justice that his coming announced and his ministry proclaimed. Amen!

Benediction

Leader: Joy to the world, the Lord is come!

People: We leave to spread this good news.

Leader: Joy to the world, the Lord is in you!

People: Thanks be to God for this immeasurable gift.

Leader: Joy to the world, the Lord will come again!

People: We will proclaim this message in our lives.

Leader: The grace of God and the sweet communion of the Holy Spirit and the love of the Child who came to die, go with you. Alleluia and amen!

CHRISTMAS · PROPER 2
Isaiah 62:6–12
Psalm 97
Titus 3:4–7
Luke 2:(1–7), 8–20

Call to Worship

Leader: The Christ Child has arrived! We have been redeemed. We have claimed his name.

People: We have been through waters and not drowned. We have been through storms and not been overwhelmed. We have been through fire and not even burned. For we belong to the Holy One of Israel, who is our help and our hope.

Leader: We are precious in God's sight, honored and loved.

People: We gather to give worthy praise for being living testimonies to the God who comes.

Call to Confession

God's faithfulness demands our response. We have failed to be worthy of God's favor.

This is our opportunity to confess, repent, and receive God's forgiveness. Shall we pray?

Confession

God, your voice calls us to relationship and our sin keeps us hidden from you. We ask your forgiveness. For we want to see you when you come again. Give us strength, we ask in the name of the Holy One, Jesus the Christ.

Words of Assurance

The voice of God calls to the four winds to gather us, to bring us back to the fold. God has called us by our individual names, created us for glory, and destined us for greatness. This is mighty good news.

Responsive Reading

Leader: The angels bow before our Majestic Creator in awe.

People: We bow in humble adoration before the Divine, whom we simply call God.

Leader: The waters, the thunder, the trees, the mountains, and every element offer praise.

People: The voice of God echoes throughout the world. There is a symphony of sounds.

Leader: There is a crescendo that arises as creatures, large and small, give their worship.

People: In this season of Christmas, we join our hearts and voices in this temple.

Leader: We give God that well-earned glory that is due.

People: God has given us strength and blessed us with inner peace. Our voices offer praise.

Offertory Invitation

Jesus came into a poor family and grew to give his all. By the sacrifice of his life, we have access to God. This is reason enough to share what we have so that others might come to know the Christ.

Offertory Praise

God, you have given us the gift of your Son, sent us the power of the Holy Spirit, called us your beloved children, and given us an inheritance among the saints. Please receive our gifts offered that we might one day soon hear you say, "You are my Beloved; with you I am well pleased." We pray in the name of the Christ.

Benediction

Leader: The little boy Samuel was given unto God's work by his mother, Hannah, for there is work for us all to do in the realm of God.

People: Jesus was born as a child of his mother, Mary, for he was the answer to the sin of the world. He has left work for all of us to do in the realm of God.

Leader: Go in the peace and power of the God who calls and empowers us to grow in favor with those we will meet this week.

People: We leave to take the spirit of Christmas into all the world. Amen.

CHRISTMAS · PROPER 3

Isaiah 52:7–10
Psalm 98
Hebrews 1:1–4, (5–12)
John 1:1–14

Call to Worship

Leader: Step lively! Step lively! God enjoys lively feet.
People: What's up with the feet and the stepping? It's Sunday morning!
Leader: So right you are, my sisters and brothers. How beautiful are the feet of those who will tell the news that our God reigns.
People: With praise upon our lips and rejoicing in our feet, we'll step lively to inform the world that Christ is born in us!

Candle Lighting

The Holy Arm of the Lord is revealed through the birth of Jesus Christ. We light this candle to announce the good news with joy!

Call to Confession

Jesus is the reflection of God's glory and the exact imprint of God's very being. With our confession of sin, that holy image is seen in us. Let us pray.

Confession

We fess up! For surely we have messed up. We've spent too much on the material stuff of this holy season. Today we ask forgiveness of the sin that controls us. Cleanse us and sustain by your Living Word, the Christ. In the name of Jesus Christ, we pray.

Words of Assurance

Long ago God spoke to our ancestors in multiple and various ways. On this Christmas Day God speaks to us by the coming of the Beloved Son. This is good news.

Responsive Reading

Leader: Turn up the decibels. Pump up the praise. It's new song time in the house!

People: We have new songs to offer unto God. For new blessings have been received. New mercy has been extended.

Leader: We have the victory! Despite situations and circumstances that appear to the contrary, this day is a shout out for victory!

People: The whole earth is glad and filled with melodies of praise.

Leader: The Maestro of Music deserves to be lifted up.

People: We will make a joyful noise unto our God. Turn up the decibels, for we are turning up the praise!

Offertory Invitation

The oil of gladness is our gift today. Let our giving reflect our grateful hearts.

Offertory Praise

God is the same. God's years will never end. For the contrast and faithful gifts we have received, we offer back a portion in thanks. To God be the glory. Amen.

Benediction

Leader: The Word is flesh.

People: The Word came to us.

Leader: The Word is flesh.

People: The Word lives among us.

Leader: The Word is flesh.

People: The Word lives in us.

Leader: Go! Be living testimonies that Jesus is alive forevermore!

People: We leave in the power of the Living Word. Amen.

FIRST SUNDAY AFTER CHRISTMAS

1 Samuel 2:18–10, 26
Psalm 148
Colossians 3:12–17
Luke 2:41–52

Call to Worship

Leader: Well, can you tell me what happened to the Christmas Spirit?
People: Didn't you hear about the Grinch who stole Christmas?
Leader: We cannot afford to let anyone or anything steal our Christmas joy!
People: You're right! We made the bills. We ate all the food. We fell into the world's trap again! Yet, God has been so faithful towards us and has come again.
Leader: People of God, we are mandated to hold fast to the Spirit of Christmas.
People: We have gathered to worship with glad hearts and with Mary's great joy. O come, let us adore him!

Lighting the Christ Candle

Letting the Spirit of Christmas dwell in us richly means that we will teach and admonish one another in all wisdom and with gratitude in our hearts sing psalms, hymns, and spiritual songs to God. And we light this candle in the name of the Lord Jesus Christ, who is coming again soon.

Call to Confession

Brothers and sisters, we have been commanded to offer righteous praise unto our God. Yet, sin has stopped our relationship with the Divine. The Spirit of Christmas demands that we stop, confess, and repent before the Most High God, who will not tolerate sin. Let us pray the prayer of confession.

Confession

Loving God, the whole earth offers praise unto you. For you commanded and all things were created. With us you took tender time and breathed life into us. And yet we have failed to do right towards you. We have sinned. Forgive us. We long to offer wholesome praise that is acceptable in your sight. You alone are exalted. We covet your amazing grace, in the name of Jesus Christ.

Words of Assurance

Bear with one another and if anyone has a complaint against another, forgive each other; just as the Lord has forgiven you, so you must also forgive. This is good news.

Responsive Reading

Leader: Worthy worship is due God.
People: Worthy worship is in heaven. Worthy worship is given by nature. Worthy worship is uplifted by the angelic host.
Leader: Worthy worship is offered by the sun and the moon.
People: Worthy worship is heard from the elements and all the creatures both great and small.
Leader: The morning stars, the evening stars, and the drifting clouds all offer God worthy praise.
People: Worthy is God, who created the heavens and the earth and maintains them by the Spoken Word.
Leader: Majestic is God, who has brought us through dangers seen and unseen. From the rising of the sun until the going down of the same, the name of our God is worthy to be praised.
People: Bring the Kwanzaa candles and light the menorah, as we lift up the cup of salvation. For we honor the Worthy God, who has brought us through the past and has great plans for our future. This day we remember the Worthy High God, who has built us as a testimony to offer praise and worthy worship! We bless the Worthy God.
Leader: People of the diaspora, God's glory is with us!
People: Praise the Lord!

Offertory Invitation

Forest fires, disappearing farms and orchards, along with drought and floods cause us great concern. But God has it all in control. We have been promised that the righteous will not be forsaken or the seed of God have to beg for bread. So we share with grateful spirits in this offering.

Offertory Praise

Great God of the tiny ant, the slumbering bears, and the seeking squirrels, we give in honor of the care you continually provide for us all. Receive these the gifts of our hands that we offer in the name of our Savior and soon coming King. Amen.

Benediction

Leader: As God's chosen ones, holy and beloved, clothe yourselves with compassion, kindness, humility, meekness, and patience. Above all, clothe yourselves with love, which binds everything together in perfect harmony. And let the peace of Christ rule in your hearts, to which you were called in one body. And be thankful.
People: We will let the Spirit of Christmas dwell in us greatly.
Leader: Go in the praise of God, the love of Christ, and the power of the Holy Spirit.
People: Amen.

WATCH NIGHT WORSHIP · DECEMBER 31

Ecclesiastes 3:1–13
Psalm 8
Matthew 25:31–46
Revelation 21:1–6

This is a service of African American congregations that began as people anticipated "watching out" the last year of slavery. The service of watching and waiting continues.

Watch night worship is a time for reflection, testimonies, and songs of God's grace. It is the period when we voice our determination for the gift of a year to come. Usually an intergenerational service, both youth and seasoned saints can play an important part. History meets the future. Tradition faces hopes. The God of the years is constant. Jesus is the same yesterday, today, and forever.

Altar Focus

A big clock with the hands stuck at five minutes to midnight sits on an altar covered with red, black, and green kente cloth. Implements such as grinders, hoes, spades, and even an old cotton sack become the visual aids. A quilt draping the altar would be another useful article. Stalks of wheat, bolls of cotton, and even tobacco leaves can be placed in vases as "floral" arrangements.

Time is optional, of course. However, the ideal gathering is around a potluck dinner with games for all ages following. Worship should begin around 10:30 P.M. Serving breakfast following worship allows the guns of salute to stop and the revelers to find their way inside!

Call to Worship

Leader: Why do we gather on this night?
People: We gather to remember our enslaved past.
Leader: Why do we gather on this night?
People: We gather to celebrate God's keeping powers.

Leader: Why do we gather on this night?

People: We gather to recall God's mercies in the midst of oppression.

Leader: Why do we gather this night?

People: We gather to celebrate our God, who journeys with us, year by year. Thanks be unto the ever faithful and true God.

Song of Praise

Call to Confession

The year is almost over. Many of the things we made covenant to do in January have fallen by the wayside. Let us seek forgiveness of our sin.

Silent Confession

Words of Assurance

Our sins are removed as far as the east is from the west. This is the promise of God. For our God yearns for authentic relationship with us. This is mighty good news.

Call to Remember

Remember God's goodness during the year. Many are the afflictions of the righteous, but the Lord delivers us from them all. Those with willingness are provided these moments to testify to the ways God has sent victory our way.

Call to Prayer for the New Year

The year is almost over. Our elders taught us how to bow on our knees before the Almighty. Kneeling conveys our humble attitude before God. Kneeling is a symbol of our grateful hearts before the throne of Grace. Let us prepare now to kneel in prayer as we watch for the New Year. Let us praise God together on our knees.

A Covenant of Declarations

Happy New Year! Thank God for another opportunity to offer praise and thanksgiving to the Maker, Redeemer, and Sustainer. Resolutions often last until after breakfast! But our foreparents made their declarations of intentions for better Christian service as they were empowered by the Holy Spirit. As you are led, please rise and state your intentions to walk with Jesus in this new year.

Offertory Invitation

Through the year God has been faithful. Our generous response through our sharing is how we say "Thanks."

Offertory Praise

Beneficent and Gracious Savior, we cannot pay for one second of the year you have brought us through. Yet, we offer these tokens in humble appreciation that as others watch and wait in the coming years, these doors will be open to receive their grateful hearts. In the name of Love, we pray.

Benediction

Leader: The old has passed and the new year has arrived.
People: We have a new beginning.
Leader: The Lord of fresh starts has given us a brand new slate.
People: We leave to write new history with our Amazing God.
Leader: Go in the peace and power of the God who holds yesterday, today, and every tomorrow. Remember, you are blessed signs of God's renewing promises as you go your way rejoicing!
People: Amen.

HOLY NAME OF JESUS DAY · JANUARY 1

Numbers 6:22–27
Psalm 8
Galatians 4:4–7 or Philippians 2:5–11
Luke 2:15–21

Call to Worship

Leader: The Name Above All Names summons us today.
People: We have heard the calling of our names.
Leader: The Name Beyond Words commands an accounting.
People: We have heard the calling of our names.
Leader: The Name Above All Names has given us a new name.
People: We bless the wonderful name of Jesus!

Call to Confession

Too often we fail to live up to the name Christian. Confession restores the worth and value of our name. Let us offer our prayers of confession.

Confession

God, you have called us by name. Like children, at times we act as if we do not hear our names being called. Forgive us our sin. Restore us to full relationship with you. We long to walk worthy of your matchless name. It is in the name of Jesus that we pray.

Words of Assurance

We have been made in the image of God. We have been crowned with glory and honor. With our confession of sin we receive restoration of the right to bear the name. Glory to the majestic name of our Sovereign God.

Responsive Reading

Leader: God's name is a household word.
People: In all places across town the name of God is uplifted.

Leader: Babies and toddlers, primary youth, and rapping teens all call on the name of God.

People: Not all talk of God is holy!

Leader: Some God language is very profane.

People: Parents call upon the name of God.

Leader: Grandparents pray the name of God.

People: Sophisticated folks tip-toe around this blessed name.

Leader: Idiots make every attempt to evade giving honor to the name of God.

People: Yet, without words, the name is spoken through the star-spangled heavens.

Leader: Without articulation the name blazes in sunrises and sunsets.

People: The breeze through the trees echoes the name.

Leader: The tiny, fragile flower, pushing its way through concrete, shouts out the name.

People: Then we look in the eyes of infants and those who are aging with grace and the matchless name is whispered again. For God's name is a household word.

Offertory Invitation

We are children of God, adopted into the royal family. We are heirs to salvation. It is our right to share in order that others may know about this wonderful relationship.

Offertory Praise

Lavishly Generous One, you have given us everything, including the right to wear the name of the Only Begotten Son. Accept these, our gifts, that others might come to wear and to bless his exalted name. In the name of Christ, we pray. Amen.

Benediction

Leader: The Lord bless you and keep you.

People: The Lord's face shine upon you.

Leader: The Lord be gracious unto you.

People: The countenance of the Lord be lifted upon you.

Leader: May the Lord, our God, grant you great shalom! Amen.

People: Hallelujah and amen.

SECOND SUNDAY AFTER CHRISTMAS

Jeremiah 31:7–14
Psalm 147:12–20
Ephesians 1:3–14
John 1:(1–9), 10–18

Call to Worship

Leader: People of God, the time has come for worship.
People: We gather to sing aloud with gladness and raise our shouts for God.
Leader: Proclaim praise and ask the Prince of Peace to save all nations.
People: For then their lives shall be like well-watered gardens and they shall not languish anymore.
Leader: The women will rejoice in the dance. The men shall have merry hearts.
People: Our mourning will be turned into joy as we receive the comfort of God. And, as we worship, every sorrow will be exchanged for gladness. For the joy of the Lord is our strength.

Call to Confession

With weeping we might have come, but with great consolation God wants us to return home. Let us offer our prayers of confession so that we might be led to the Spring of Living Waters. Let us confess our sin.

Confession

God, you were gracious enough to send Jesus Christ to break the bands of sin that Satan held over us. He brought us redemption and we have continued in sin. Forgive us, we pray in his atoning name.

Words of Assurance

In Jesus Christ God provides ransom and pardon. Jesus is the Good Shepherd and we have access to him by the mere words of our confession. By grace we are saved. This is good news!

Responsive Reading

Leader: God is worthy! God is worthy! God is worthy of our praise.
People: God's grace and strength have carried us through another week.
Leader: Our children have been blessed. God's mercy keeps them covered.
People: God's Word is alive in our midst. We stand on the promises and refuse to simply exist on the premises.
Leader: The seasons are faithful, reminding us of God's steadfast love.
People: Who can stand before the awesome God?
Leader: The elements sing of God's glory. Every season has its song of praise.
People: God's Word is faithful and true. The promise is that the last shall be first. It is our time! Worthy is our God!

Offertory Invitation

In the beginning was the Word, and the Word was with God, and the Word was God. With grateful hearts let us share, that the Word may continue to be spread.

Offertory Praise

True Light, who enlightens everyone, we appreciate your coming into the world. Receive these our meager gifts. In the name of the Light of the World, we pray.

Benediction

Leader: The Word has become flesh and has come to live among us.
People: We are the light of the world.
Leader: The world needs to see and to know the Light.
People: We are the light of the world.
Leader: The Word is flesh and lives in you.
People: We are the light of the world! It is so, now and forever more.

3 · THE SEASON OF EPIPHANY

The Greco-Roman world gave us the word *epiphany*. Epiphany designated for them the occasion when state officials made public appearances within the provinces. The early Church adopted the term to indicate the manifestations of Christ within the world. During Epiphany we get different snapshots of the Savior's brilliant glory.

The Greek word *epiphaneia* means to manifest, show forth, or make clear. The bright star of Bethlehem guided the Wise to get a glimpse of the newborn Sovereign. During this season of illumination, many sightings of the Divine will help us view the many-faceted aspects of our great Savior and the plan for our salvation.

January 6 is the official Feast of Epiphany. This date signals the arrival of the known world to give honor and treasure to Jesus and also signifies his baptism by John, when the full Trinity is displayed.

The intent of the month of January in general is new beginnings, fresh starts, and the additional opportunities God supplies for us. Its theme can be the light of justice. Epiphany, baptismal renewal, and the Dr. Martin Luther King Jr. celebration are priorities of this month.

Altar Focus

To symbolize light, a large, old-fashioned kerosene lamp can be the altar focus for the first Sunday in January. A menorah, with black, red, and green candles, can be placed between the usual Christ candles. When Epiphany is celebrated on the Sunday nearest January 6, the altar focus can feature water pitchers of various shapes and sizes, goblets, crystal decanters, and treasure chests. This is another liturgical day of white, and gold stars will enhance the world's "illumination."

On the Sunday that reaffirmation of baptism is celebrated, a large, clear, crystal bowl filled with water or one of the "heritage" wash basins, and pitchers can be featured. Conch shells, dried sponges, and assorted sea shells call out, "Take me to the water!" The baptismal font and other symbols of baptism are welcomed. The Sunday nearest January 6 is the opportune day for celebrating baptismal renewal.

For Dr. King's celebration, a grapevine wreath may be the altar focus, wrapped in black, red, and green cloth or paper, with large red flowers having yellow centers, to represent our homeland and our continuing struggle for liberty and justice. The altar need not be fully changed weekly, but enhanced for the particular liturgical setting of worship.

EPIPHANY

Isaiah 60:1–6
Psalm 72:1–7, 10–14
Ephesians 3:1–12
Matthew 2:1–12

Call to Worship

Leader: Have you not heard? Did you not know? Christ went to Africa!
People: What in the world do you mean?
Leader: God sent the Light of the World to Africa!
People: Why did this happen?
Leader: The spirit of death was seeking to extinguish the Light. Africa was hospitable and welcomed her son home.
People: Let's give the Radiant God praise for a goodly land that provided refuge for the Hope of the World!

Call to Confession

The Light has come, and too often we refuse to acknowledge its presence. Let us confess our preference for the absence of illumination.

Confession

Lord of light and ability to see, we confess our sin of ignoring you and refusing to open our eyes to your radiance. Your light causes us to look inward to change, and not outward to blame others. Your light pulls us up to action instead of down in hopelessness. Your light means transformation and change. Your light scares us! Forgive us, we pray, for our sin.

Words of Assurance

Lift up your eyes and look around; the glory of the Lord shines on you and in you! Your sons and your daughters shall see and be radiant! Your heart shall thrill and rejoice, because abundance and the wealth of nations shall come to you (Isaiah 60). Praise the Lord!

Responsive Reading

Leader: Warrior God, we praise you for the reign of your son.
People: He came to judge the poor with justice and your inheritance with righteousness.

Leader: We continue to pray that Jesus Christ will defeat our foes, root out systems of poverty, and send us deliverance from every oppressor.
People: Jesus, our elder brother, has lived among us since the generations of the ancestors.
Leader: May his loving ways be like fresh rain, which showers the earth and its inhabitants.
People: Our hearts long for his reign of right living and abiding peace.
Leader: May the world's leaders render their hearts to his leading. May the rulers of every province and tribe bring the sacrifice of their willing spirits. May the wealthy and the greedy bow before him in reverence and in honor.
People: For their hearts are yet in God's hands. And without God we have no help.
Leader: We have received mercy from God in our past.
People: From oppression and violence, God has redeemed our life. Those who have died struggling for justice are precious in the sight of our God. God preserves the lives of those who are in need!

Offertory Invitation

The wise of every generation know to open their treasures to the Inspiration of Glory. The Wise offered what they had. This privilege is ours today.

Offertory Praise

Jesus Christ came and opened his treasure chest of inheritance unto us. Now we have access to God and boldness and confidence through faith in him. So that the world might know this birthright, we offer what is ours. In the name of the Giver, we pray.

Benediction

Leader: The star is yet shining and people are yet looking for the Light of the World!
People: We leave to point the way.
Leader: The manger is empty, and the angelic choir no longer sings.
People: Christ is at home in our hearts! His song of victory is on our lips.
Leader: The light of Christ will lead you, the love of Christ will enfold you, and the spirit of Christ will live through you, world without end! Amen and amen!

FIRST SUNDAY AFTER EPIPHANY · BAPTISM OF THE LORD

Isaiah 43:1–7
Psalm 29
Acts 8:14–17
Luke 3:15–17, 21–22

Call to Worship

Leader: This is a day to recall God's love affair with water!
People: This is a day to remember our baptisms with thankfulness.
Leader: This is a day to recall the embryonic fluids of our birth.
People: This is a day of great thanksgiving to the God who loves water!

Call to Confession

In the beginning God called and chaos gave way to order and beauty. This Lord's Day is our call for the sinful chaos in our life to give way with our confession. Let us turn to God.

Confession

Great God, we have heard your call to move from the disorder of our lives. We have gathered because we cannot do it alone. We come to ask your forgiveness of our sin. Wash us clean. Remove our bent toward sin and sinfulness. Give us willing hearts to follow you, your Word, and your divine way. Mark us afresh this day with the washing of your Holy Spirit, we pray in the matchless name of the Christ Child, who was born to die in our place. May it be so now and always.

Words of Assurance

The voice of God thunders over the waters. And the voice of God speaks forgiveness to our parched and weary spirits. This is mighty good news.

Responsive Reading

Leader: God, we join with the angels and call out a shout of "Bravo!"
People: We have come to offer our meager worship to you who are robed in holy splendor.

Leader: We have come dressed in our best and realize that our inner lives are as filthy rags before your holiness.

People: As we enter this sacred place, your holiness overwhelms us and we see our need for cleansing.

Leader: In this sanctuary the voice of God thunders!

People: The brilliant holiness of God thunders throughout the earth.

Leader: We stand in awe before the magnificent greatness of God.

People: The symphonic thunders of God call out reminders of God's majesty.

Leader: It is God who thunders over the waters.

People: God's thunder smashes, skips, topples, jumps, and sets trees to dancing.

Leader: God's thunder invites, enfolds, baptizes, dips, sprinkles, gushes, and enmeshes us into the mystery of our faith.

People: The God of thundering and still waters gives all people shalom!

Offertory Invitation

John baptized with the waters of repentance, telling people to believe in Jesus Christ, who was to come. Jesus has come. We have found deliverance from our sin. Our giving makes room for others to come and to believe. Let's share in this hope.

Offertory Praise

People across the world have the invitation to come and be baptized in the name of Jesus Christ. With our offerings we give thanks for the privilege of spreading this good news. In the name of the Beloved, we pray.

Benediction

Leader: Leave! Remember your baptism has named you Beloved.

People: We go to take our new name in action throughout the world we touch.

Leader: Leave! Remember your baptism has claimed you as an heir.

People: We go to live as those who have the inheritance of Love within their hearts.

Leader: Leave! Remember your baptism has given you access to the keeping power of the Holy Spirit! Walk in creative power. Act with holy boldness. Touch the world gently with the Amazing Grace of one baptized into the Royal Family. Amen!

SECOND SUNDAY AFTER EPIPHANY

Isaiah 62:1–5
Psalm 36:5–10
1 Corinthians 12:1–11
John 2:1–11

Call to Worship

Leader: The search continues. The call is out. God is looking for those who will represent.

People: Here I am, Lord, send me.

Leader: There are people crying. There are people dying. There are people who need hope.

People: Here I am, Lord, send me.

Leader: There is much depression, much despair, much pain.

People: Here I am, Lord, send me.

Leader: In this season of Epiphany, God is searching for those who will twinkle in their places.

People: We have heard your call. Speak, your servants are listening.

Call to Confession

The noise of this world makes us deaf to the small, still, and quiet voice of the Holy One. In these sacred moments we can confess our sin and listen for God as the inner clamor ceases. Let us center down.

Silent Confession

Confession

God, we confess that too often we do not hear you call. The real deal is that we get so busy doing our own thing that we forget to listen! Yet, we long to hear a fresh word from you. Forgive us our sin. Speak to our hearts.

Words of Assurance

Hear the good news. Confession clears our hearts and opens our ears. God has already spoken words of forgiveness and amazing grace.

Responsive Reading

Leader: God the investigator has been on the case!

People: God knows all the facts of our lives. They are not all good!

Leader: Our lives are like open books to God.

People: Before we speak, the thoughts we think are revealed unto God.

Leader: We cannot escape the clutches of the Almighty.

People: We are never out of God's sight.

Leader: When we leave, when we get back, is insignificant, for God already has the news.

People: It's overwhelming to realize that there is no spot where God is not!

Leader: It's mind boggling to recognize that God encompasses all we say, think, or do.

People: It's reassuring to come to grips with the reality that God is always near.

Leader: God knew us before we were formed in our mother's womb.

People: We are wonderful! We are awesome! We are made in the image of the Divine.

Offertory Invitation

God's thoughts toward us are more than the grains of sand. We cannot count the many and various ways that God works on our behalf. Let us show our inadequate appreciation by sharing with others.

Offertory Praise

High God, receive these our tokens of gratitude in thanks for all you do for us. May these offerings be used to spread your name, your power, and your glory throughout the earth. We pray in the name of your son, Jesus.

Benediction

Leader: Leave to be the Church everywhere you go!

People: We leave knowing that we have been called to be sent to bring others.

Leader: Leave remembering that you are wonderful!

People: We leave in the knowledge of whose we are—wonderful offspring of a Wonder-Working God! This is truly our good news! Amen.

THIRD SUNDAY AFTER EPIPHANY

Nehemiah 8:1–3, 5–6, 8–10
Psalm 19
1 Corinthians 12:12–31a
Luke 4:14–21

Call to Worship

Leader: The Light of Epiphany shines upon the Living Word!
People: We have come to worship and to gain new wisdom and understanding
Leader: This is the first day of a new week. The Word of God will be read and heard with clarity.
People: Let the ears of all the people be attentive. God has a fresh word for both the young and old.
Leader: This day is holy unto the Lord, our God; we will not mourn or weep.
People: Together we will bless the Great God with praise, as we lift up holy hands. Amen. Amen.

Call to Confession

Like the children of Israel, we come week after week to hear a message of love. Then we leave this sacred place and neglect to live sacred lives. This is our time for confession. Let us pray.

Confession

Spirit of the Living God, you have anointed us to carry good news, and we have carried lies and gossip. You told us to take good news to the poor, and we have too often turned away from them. You sent us to proclaim release to captives, to allow the oppressed to go free, and we have become greater oppressors ourselves. You called us to proclaim that this was the year of your favor, and we have lifted up our own name instead of yours. Forgive us our sin. Give us your saving grace, we pray, in the name of your Son, Jesus.

Words of Assurance

Now we are the body of Christ and individually members of it. God has appointed us to be apostles, prophets, teachers, powerful healers, helpers, leaders, and those who speak with new tongues. This is good news. Thanks be unto God.

Responsive Reading

Leader: There is an exhibit of God's wonders on display throughout the universe.

People: The creative voice of God has designed splendid crafts for our pleasure.

Leader: God's sun and moon hold court daily. The stars of the heavens twinkle and flash.

People: The elements were not given voice, but their beauty speaks for them.

Leader: Silence bows in homage before the magnificent wonders performed by God.

People: From the rising of the sun, through the swaying of the trees, the seasons that march in order, and the seas that never forget their course, God's Word is alive and well.

Leader: The desert rose, the mighty Alps, the icebergs of Alaska, the seven wonders of the world, and the most tiny daisy, awaiting its turn to bloom, all bring faith alive in our hearts.

People: Our hearts are warmed at the thought of God having ordered all these marvelous things just for us! Everything our human eyes can see points us anew to the One who was and is and is to come. We offer thanks for signs of God everywhere.

Offertory Invitation

The Word of God calls us to "Go our way, eat the fat of the land and drink sweet wine and send portions of them to those for whom nothing is prepared, for this day is holy to the Lord, our God." Our sharing in this offering helps us to keep God's Light shining in the whole world.

Offertory Praise

Let the words of our mouths and the meditations of our hearts be acceptable unto you, O Lord, our Rock and our Redeemer. We thank you for this opportunity to share with others as we have given, and we pray in the matchless name of Jesus Christ.

Benediction

Leader: The law of the Lord is perfect, reviving the soul.
People: The decrees of the Lord are sure, making wise the simple.
Leader: The precepts of the Lord are right, bringing joy to our hearts.
People: The commandment of the Lord is clear, enlightening the eyes.
Leader: The reverence of the Lord is pure, enduring forever.
People: The ordinances of the Lord are true and righteous altogether.
Leader: They are more to be desired than gold, even much fine gold!
People: God's Word is sweeter than honey, and drippings of the honeycomb.
Leader: Go! Be a sunbeam in everything you do! The Epiphany is in your hands. Amen.

FOURTH SUNDAY AFTER EPIPHANY

Jeremiah 1:4–10
Psalm 71:1–6
1 Corinthians 13:1–13
Luke 4:21–30

Call to Worship

Leader: The frightened, the ill, the afflicted, the single, working mom and children are welcomed into the presence of the Almighty this day.
People: This is the place for all who feel left out, dismayed, and alone.
Leader: In this sanctuary, there is help, hope, and healing.
People: We have gathered for renewal as we worship.
Leader: None is too young or too old to be touched by the Anointing God.
People: The Light of the Nations has called. We gather with glad sounds of praise. In the God of refuge, we worship the Holy Spirit and the Truth.

Call to Confession

The Word of Life appeals to us to love one another. We are aware of how messed up our relationships have become. Love is a healing balm. Let us confess our sin and repent so that Love may work in and among us.

Confession

Lover of our souls, we approach your throne with prayers of confession. We have not lived up to your aim for our lives. We have not been patient or kind; we have been envious, boastful, and rude. We do insist upon our own ways. We are irritable and resentful, and we rejoice in wrong. We are sinners. We need your amazing grace. Forgive us, we pray, in the name of him who first loved us. Amen.

Words of Assurance

Now we see in a mirror dimly, but soon we will see God face to face. Now we know only in part, but soon we will know God fully, even as we will be fully known. And now faith, hope, and love abide, these three. The greatest of these is love. Sisters and brothers, this is good news. Thanks be to God.

Responsive Reading

Leader: Like a little child being hunted by the neighborhood bully, we can run to God for safety.

People: Our lives are testimonies that God gets the glory for keeping us alive.

Leader: God leans close to hear our complaints. God comes close to wipe our weeping eyes.

People: It is God who has picked us up, time after time, and established our way again.

Leader: The door to the Heart of Hope is forever open.

People: We have never been turned away or left to fight all alone.

Leader: Even when the going has been really rough, God has stood by our side.

People: We have this sure testimony that our God cares and provides.

Leader: From our most early existence up to this very present moment, God has been our fortress.

People: The ancestors gave us the bedrock of their faith. We will be held by God's eternal hand.

Offertory Invitation

God has been our rock of refuge, our strong tower, a pillar of defense, and a present help in every trouble. We have been rescued from the hand of the wicked and snatched from the grasp of the unjust and the cruel. We cannot repay God. The only thing we can do is to share God's goodness with others as we give as unto the Ancient of Days.

Offertory Praise

God, you have appointed us over nations and kingdoms, to pluck up and to pull down, to destroy and to overthrow, in order that you might build and plant. We have given our thanksgivings in monetary measures. Please accept them in the name of the Light who yet shines throughout the world.

Benediction

Leader: During the famine in the African town of Zarephath in Sidon, Elijah the prophet was sent by God to the home of a poor, single, working mom for food.

People: Prophets are not well received in their home towns.

Leader: She didn't have the bread that the prophet asked her for, but she had the necessary ingredients and a willing attitude to share what she owned with a stranger.

People: Prophets are not well received in their home towns.

Leader: Her willingness to obey and to share fed her and the prophet and her son all the days of the famine.

People: She became a shining example of God's light to the "strange prophet" in town. We leave to trust God and to obey, sharing as we go. Hallelujah and amen!

FIFTH SUNDAY AFTER EPIPHANY

Isaiah 6:1–8, (9–13)
Psalm 138
1 Corinthians 15:1–11
Luke 5:1–11

Call to Worship

Leader: The God of All Knowledge awaits our arrival this morning.
People: It is a struggle to come into the presence of a Holy God with our baggage.
Leader: Bring your imperfections and your sin. God is calling today.
People: Will God receive us who recognize our ugly ways and want to change?
Leader: The All Knowing yearns for our true relationship.
People: We come with all of our "stuff" to offer the Worthy and Holy God our worship and praise.

Call to Confession

The voices of the angels sing "Holy, Holy, Holy" to the One who sits upon the throne. Yet we are aware that sin separates us from offering pure praise. With repentant hearts let us pray.

Confession

Woe is me. I am lost, for I am one with unclean lips, and I live among people of unclean lips. Yet my eyes have seen the beauty of holiness and I desire to be clean. Forgive me, God, I pray in the name of Purifying Fire.

Words of Assurance

Leader: Now that confession has touched your lips, your guilt has departed and your sin is blotted out. Whom shall God send? Who will go and shine for the Almighty God?
People: Here I am, God of Hosts. Send me, I'll go. Amen.

Responsive Reading

Leader: Melodies from heaven reverberate throughout our lives.
People: The Almighty does so many great things that words cannot express our awe.

Leader: Many times God answers before we call and comes before we know help is needed.

People: When we find ourselves humming wordless tunes it is because deliverance has appeared.

Leader: Music is a gift from beyond ourselves that slips into us to lift our spirits.

People: Chords of strength and scales of great mercy drop into our hearts without words.

Leader: We sing because we refuse to be destroyed!

People: Truthfully we sing because the Deliverer has worked on our behalf. All we can offer is a song of praise that is woefully inadequate.

Leader: The powerful and immutable One encourages us with notes beyond paper.

People: God, tune our hearts to the perfect pitch of true worship of your majesty.

Leader: Sing of God's wonders, delight in God's presence, be thankful for God's mighty acts.

People: We sing songs of gratitude to our faithful God! Hallelujah! Praise to Jehovah!

Offertory Invitation

Because God is great in strength and mighty in power, no one who calls in faith will be turned away. God is calling us by name. Let us share our resources to ensure that the call is heard around the world.

Offertory Praise

God, you have given us such a great reward, the gift of salvation. You gave it to us free of charge. We offer our gifts for the sake of the gospel that all may share in its blessings. Receive them in the name of Jesus Christ.

Benediction

Leader: People are yet searching for signs of the Christ.

People: We return to our neighborhoods, our schools, our jobs, and our homes to share the good news. We want the world to see Jesus in our lives!

Leader: Jesus didn't travel far, but the message of salvation spread.

People: Wherever we go, the good news will be shared!

Leader: Go! The commission to make new disciples is ours. And the power belongs to us! Amen.

SIXTH SUNDAY AFTER EPIPHANY

Jeremiah 17:5–10
Psalm 1
1 Corinthians 15:12–20
Luke 6:17–26

Call to Worship

Leader: God, the tester of hearts and searcher of our minds, calls us to gather.
People: God, the regulator of minds and the stabilizer of spirits, you have our attention.
Leader: God, the planter of thoughts and the organizer of every good deed, is present to us.
People: God, the Way Maker and the one who opens closed doors, is our help and our hope. This is our time. The hour has come. The heavens await our praise.

Call to Confession

God has told us that our hearts are devious above all else. As a matter of fact, they are perverse, and surely we cannot comprehend why we do the things that we do. It's time for confession.

Confession

God, we are cursed with the sin of rebellion. We are like shrubs in the desert without evidence of holy living. Forgive us. Restore us to fruitful living.

Words of Assurance

Blessed are those who trust in God. They shall be like trees planted by water, sending out its roots by the stream. This is good news. Thanks be to God.

Responsive Reading

Leader: The Divine Counselor knows that we are enticed by evil.

People: We live in association with evildoers.

Leader: God has given us sure direction to places of rest.

People: To be blessed means to bloom where we are planted.

Leader: The One who knows our way offers us life-giving ability if we live by the Living Word.

People: Trusting in God is a learned ability. Following after God means having a true resource.

Leader: Chew on the Word. Digest the Word. Green pastures are provided in the midst of the deserts.

People: We are living trees of refreshment and the world needs us.

Leader: Life cannot blow us in the wind, for we have an anchor in the Wellspring of Life.

People: We have joy in the struggles of life, for we know deep roots in the Eternal God.

Offertory Invitation

Jesus is Lord to the glory of God. This is our faith and our sure confidence. We are in covenant to spread this news to the world. By our giving, the Light will shine in places we will never visit. Let's give as unto God.

Offertory Praise

God, blessed are the poor, who will receive the realm of God. Blessed are the weepers, for soon they will laugh. Blessed are the hungry, who will be filled to overflowing. For we have given to ensure that your Word is fulfilled through us. We appreciate the opportunity to share in the name of the One whom you sent to save us. Amen.

Benediction

Leader: Twinkle, twinkle little stars! Go! Be an epiphany of the Christ!

People: Our God knows who we really are, attitude, faults, and all. Yet, we are sent to shine in all the places we go this week.

Leader: Proclaim Christ as risen from the dead.

People: We will testify to his resurrection power in our lives.

Leader: Go in the name of the Restoring Creator, with the victory of rising and the power of being kept!

People: Hallelujah and amen!

SEVENTH SUNDAY AFTER EPIPHANY

Genesis 45:3–11, 15
Psalm 37:1–11, 39–40
1 Corinthians 15:35–38, 42–50
Luke 6:27–38

Call to Worship

Leader: This is a day of difficult sayings. God's Word will cut us today!
People: We have heard harsh words all week. Speak to us about a gentle Savior.
Leader: The Words of Life are not always soft and sweet. They come to cut through our stuff.
People: We want to be soothed and comforted when we come to worship.
Leader: Being given false hope will not keep us when the difficulties of life come knocking.
People: When will God get rid of evil and troublemakers?
Leader: That is a question reserved for God's timing and the second coming of Jesus Christ.
People: We have gathered so that we might be ready when the Light of the World returns. We open our hearts and our ears to hear authentic Truth and to worship with honest praise.

Call to Confession

Jesus commanded us to "Love your enemies. Do good to those who hate you. Bless those who curse you. Pray for those who abuse you. Give to everyone who begs from you, and if anyone takes away your goods, do not ask for them again. Do to others as you would have them do unto you." We have failed to follow the way of Jesus Christ. Let us repent.

Confession

God, we have been drawn away by the desires of our hearts and the lust of our own spirits. Like the brothers of Joseph we have been caught wrong, trying to destroy others, being jealous, and lying to cover our sin.

We have failed to follow in the footsteps of the Christ. Forgive us. Cleanse us. In the name of the One who delivers from every pit in life, we pray.

Words of Assurance

When we trust in God and do good we will live and enjoy security. Let us take delight in God, who will give us the desires of our hearts. This is good news.

Responsive Reading

Leader: Don't get hung up on those who seem to prosper in doing wrong.
People: We see their wicked deeds and their seeming accumulation of "things," while we work and seem to have so little to show for our right living.
Leader: The promise of God is that what they desire will come in due season. Like the grass clippings and wilted flowers that fade away, their time is short and known by God.
People: There is a blessed assurance that we have seen over and over in our lives, so we stick with God.
Leader: God holds everything and wants to share with those who live within divine grace.
People: When we don't hold back on God, we are guaranteed that God will not withhold from us.
Leader: The sunshine testifies and the moonlight glows to show evidence of God's faithfulness in the whole world.
People: We try hard not to get caught up in the struggle to succeed according to the standards of the world.
Leader: God does not treat success like we do. We are not called to be successful, but we are called to be faithful.
People: Being faithful doesn't offer quick and easy promotions and offer us the fame and fortune that get headlines. Sometimes faithful living gets us called ugly names, for it seems as if we are doing nothing.
Leader: Prayer is effective. Prayer is essential. Prayer is doing what God desires of us. By prayer we are connected with every divine resource and angelic assistance in every battle. Keep praying.
People: Thank God for keeping an accurate record of our hearts' motivation. For in the long run, we will stand before the Great Judge and reap our eternal success. This is our faith.

Offertory Invitation

The salvation of the righteous is from our God, who is our refuge in the time of trouble. Our faith is in the same God who has proved to be present to help and to rescue. Because we have a safe haven and the abundance of the heavenlies as our resource, we can share with gratitude.

Offertory Praise

God, you promised that if we would give, it would be given back to us. You guaranteed that a good measure of return, pressed down, shaken together, and running over, will come into our laps—for the measure that we give will be the measure that we receive back. Our laps are open for the overflow that we have given in the name of the One who gave all for us.

Benediction

Leader: Go into the world and show mercy this week.
People: We will be the divine reflections of Christ and twinkle in the places that we touch.
Leader: Go into the world and do not judge this week.
People: We will be the soft answers and the gentle response in showing the world Christ this week.
Leader: Go into the world and be love this week.
People: We will love the unlovable and be kind to the wicked and the ungrateful.
Leader: The boldness of God, the gentleness of Christ, and the ready help of the Holy Spirit go with us as we go to be epiphanies of the Living Hope of the World!
People: Hallelujah and amen.

EIGHTH SUNDAY AFTER EPIPHANY

Isaiah 55:10–13
Psalm 92:1–4, 12–15
1 Corinthians 15:51–58
Luke 6:39–49

Call to Worship

Leader: Listen, I will tell you a mystery! We shall not all die, but we will all be changed.
People: In a moment, in the twinkling of an eye, at the last trumpet sound, the dead will be raised imperishable, and we will be changed.
Leader: For our perishable body must put on imperishability.
People: And this mortal body must put on immortality so that the saying that is written will be fulfilled: "Death has been swallowed up in victory. Where, O death, is your victory? Where, O grave, is your sting?"
Leader: The sting of death is sin. And the power of sin is the law.
People: But thanks be to God, who gives us the victory through Christ!

Call to Confession

God hears our feeble cries and rushes to bring us comfort. God's eye roams the world seeking those who live lives worthy of favor. Yet sin keeps us separate from a loving God. This is our opportunity to seek forgiveness.

Confession

Provider God, we gather to offer thanks and praise for all you have done for us in the past week. We stop now to confess that we have not loved you back in kind. We have failed to keep your laws and to love ourselves or our neighbors in ways that show your reign in us. Forgive our sin, we pray in the name of the One who loves us best, Jesus the Christ.

Words of Assurance

As the rain and the snow come down from heaven and do not return there until they have watered the earth, making it bring forth and sprout, giving seed to the sower and bread to the eater, so shall the Living Word of God that goes out and is received. That Word shall not return empty to God, but will succeed for the sanctification of our souls. This is good news.

Responsive Reading

Leader: People of God, we have an inexhaustible well within us that primes the faith that belonged to our ancestors.
People: Their spirituals have sustained our faith.
Leader: People of God, when we think of God's goodness, faithfulness, and encompassing love, an appropriate hymn addresses our thanksgiving
People: Our hymns address the benevolence of the Almighty.
Leader: The world joins in with chords of harmony.
People: God continues to comprehend the music of our tears.
Leader: We sing our faith songs to remind us of the faithfulness of God.
People: We have been young. Some of us have aged. Yet, God has never failed to sustain us. Therefore, we make melodies in our hearts unto God.

Offertory Invitation

Beloved, we are called to be steadfast, immovable, always excelling in the work of God, because we know that none of our labor is in vain on behalf of the Light of the World. So let's give to do our part, ensuring that the Light glows everywhere.

Offertory Praise

Generous God, how we thank you for the opportunity to share from resources you have lovingly provided. Accept now our sacrificial giving in the name of the One who brought us victory over sin, hell, and death, we pray.

Benediction

Leader: Go out in joy, knowing that God will keep you in peace.
People: With all of nature, we go forth in songs of praise.
Leader: For your song, God will give you increase.
People: We leave, singing love songs to God.
Leader: Go in the power of God, the Rock of our salvation; of Jesus Christ, the music to our ears; and of the mysterious Holy Spirit, who will sing through us as we go!
People: Hallelujah and amen.

NINTH SUNDAY AFTER EPIPHANY

1 Kings 8:22–23, 41–43
Psalm 96:1–9
Galatians 1:1–12
Luke 7:1–10

Call to Worship

Leader: There is no God like ours, who keeps covenant and steadfast love for all who walk right.
People: With a great name, a mighty hand, and an outstretched arm, our God is known to all the people of the earth.
Leader: The name of God is invoked in this place.
People: The name of God is invoked in us, temples of the Living God.
Leader: This day we join with people across the world who call upon the name of our God.
People: With reverence and awe we come to offer glory to the Most High in our worship.
Yesterday, today, and forever more, the name of God is worthy to be praised.

Call to Confession

Great is the Lord, our God, and greatly to be praised by those with pure hearts and right spirits. Let us use this time to prepare our hearts for true worship through confession.

Confession

God, we have spent the past week seeking the approval of so many other small gods. We have bowed before their altars and given them your worship. Forgive our sin. Cleanse our sin from us. Make us fit to worship you in spirit and in truth. We pray in the name of your Only Begotten Son.

Words of Assurance

Leader: Peace to you and peace from God, our Creator, and the Lord Jesus Christ, who gave himself for our sins to set us free from the present evil age, according to the will of God, to whom be glory forever and ever.
People: Amen and amen.

Responsive Reading

Leader: God of the troubled and confused, today we feel like singing the blues.
People: The terror, the downsizing, the violence, and the laws of scarce resources leave us with notes of discord and disharmony.
Leader: Peace beyond comprehension belongs to us in the very time of horror and discontentment.
People: Fresh mercies bring fresh notes of thanksgiving to mind.
Leader: The Holy Guide of the discomforted leads us to ways of singing in the face of evil.
People: We need a new anointing to fall upon us so that our new songs will be pleasant sounds to God.
Leader: The dew of the morning and the light of this day call forth new notes of praise.
People: We do not serve an idol god but a great God who is the source of our salvation.
Leader: Honor, power, majesty, and might belong to our God.
People: We bring the meditation of our mouths and the sacrifices of our hearts as melodies of love.
Leader: Give out a shout for the Almighty.
People: We come into the courts of the Most High with songs of delight and worship in adoration.

Offertory Invitation

If we were still pleasing people, we would not be servants of Christ. But we have come to recognize that the gospel was not proclaimed by a mere human source, but through the sacrificial giving of Jesus Christ at Calvary. Therefore, we can share, knowing that we give only because he gave first. It is now our turn.

Offertory Praise

God, you love us and provided for us this place that we call by your name. In many places, plenty of people have not this sacred privilege. Therefore, we pray that what we have given might be a blessing of Light to those who need to know you in material as well as spiritual ways. We offer these gifts in the name of the Giver of Light.

Benediction

May the Caring God go before you to light your way. May the Healing God go before you to make your way plain. May the God of resurrection keep you getting up whenever you fall down. And may God, our Great Shalom, surround you and give you great joy as you journey through the week. God the Way Maker, Jesus the Way, and the Holy Spirit, your company keeper, go with and before you.

LAST SUNDAY AFTER EPIPHANY · TRANSFIGURATION SUNDAY

Exodus 34:29–35
Psalm 99
2 Corinthians 3:12–4:2
Luke 9:28–36, (37–43)

Call to Worship

Leader: Now the Lord is the Spirit, and where the Spirit of the Lord is, there is freedom.
People: And all of us with unveiled faces come to seek the glory of the Lord.
Leader: The glory of God seen as through a mirror is being transformed into the same image from one degree of glory to another, for this comes from the Holy Spirit.
People: Therefore, since it is by God's mercy that we are engaged in this ministry, we do not lose hope. We have renounced the shameful things that one hides; we refuse to practice deceit or make false God's Word. But by the open statement of our faith we commend ourselves to the conscience of everyone in the sight of God. We long for the world to see God reflected in our lives. For this reason we have come with every intent to worship Christ our Savior.

Call to Confession

Moses tried to fool the children of Israel by hiding behind a veil. He didn't want them to see that God's glory was rapidly fading from his features like a suntan in cold weather. But the people saw that he was not God! People have seen the ungod in us this week. It's time to take off our veils of un-righteousness and go quickly to confession.

Confession

God of the Epiphany, we have indeed seen your glory radiate throughout this season. We have seen you in both large and small ways, in both young and in old. However, we recognize that we have not always reflected you honestly before the world. We have sinned and made you look really bad.

We confess to the sin within us. Forgive us. Restore us, we pray, in the name of the Lamb who came to take away our sin.

Words of Assurance

The Lord our God is an answering and forgiving God who also avenges us of our wrongdoings through the shed blood of Jesus Christ. This is our good news!

Responsive Reading

Leader: We want to see the One who is exalted above the heavens and the earth.

People: We cannot see the face of God and live. For our God is a consuming fire. Moses could only see his hind parts and the brilliance was overwhelming.

Leader: We see God in the multiple ways that love makes itself manifest in our world. We are the visible images of God in the world.

People: The change in us has been amazing. What we were before is gone. And what we can be only God knows. For we have a divine and awesome future that is hidden in the mystery of God.

Leader: We worship an awesome God who does not hide upon a mountain, but has come low enough to be experienced in the transformation of our little lives.

People: O how we worship the God who comes to see about those who call in faith. This God has come as a pillar of cloud and fire. This God has come as a rock and a wheel. This God has come as a child and a dying man. This God has come as Light to all the nations. The name of the Lord is a high tower and we, the saints, run to the sanctuary to lift our hands in holy worship.

Offertory Invitation

Only the chosen ones were offered the opportunity to go with Jesus to the mountain to pray. As they watched, the appearance of his face changed and his clothes became dazzling. The disciples wanted to remain there in buildings made by hand. But the realm of God is among us. And all of us can be part of its being built as we share!

Offertory Praise

God, our Provider, we are those called to be your agents in this world. May this offering change the lives of many, we pray. Receive now these gifts given to heal, restore, bless, and set captives free. We give them in response to the change you have made in our lives as we offer thanks in the name of Compassion.

Benediction

Leader: Friends of God, leave to be agents of change in the world.
People: We are changed to be change agents.
Leader: Disciples of Christ, leave to be glorious workers with him everywhere you go.
People: We have undergone interior change so that we can be effective workers beyond these walls.
Leader: Bearers of the Holy Spirit, be mighty in the Spirit so that miracles and wonders will happen through you.
People: We are broken vessels willing to overflow with the goodness we have received.
Leader: We have a divine destiny, a changed future, and an inspiring week as we work the work of the One who is sending us to be wonder workers.
People: The mission is not impossible. We have been transformed. Thanks be to God. Hallelujah and amen.

4 · THE SEASON OF LENT

We become pilgrims on the forty-day journey, seeking our way out of the wilderness of sin in the season of Lent. It is a serious period of spiritual discipline as we either give up something pleasant or take on a new mission to enable others. Lent is our individual struggle to subdue our flesh and to wrestle with the sin issue, which tempts us so readily.

The early church prepared new members, catechumens, for Easter Sunday baptism. There was an intense year of being indoctrinated into the faith community. Both instructors and students of the faith fasted, prayed, studied, and made themselves more consciously aware of the sacrifice of Jesus Christ.

The Israelites wandered forty years in the wilderness. Jesus spent forty days and nights struggling with Satan in the wilderness. We will journey through our own forty-day wilderness, knowing that resurrection is on the way.

It is good to note that Sundays are not included in the forty-day Lenten period. For each Sunday worship experience is a reenactment of the resurrection!

Altar Focus

As the drama of Lent unfolds with its journey toward the cross and resurrection, the altar should set the tempo for meditation and reflection. A Lenten garden might be a possibility for you. Local florists will gather the necessary plants and rent them for the season. Included should be any plant that will remind us of the Garden of Gethsemane, the place where Jesus spent his hours anticipating death for us.

Stalks of wheat and vines should be heavily emphasized, as Jesus is the Bread of Life and the Vine from which we are nourished. Wheat was most likely the most important crop in that period. A huge rock or simulated boulder should be included to remind us of wise and foolish persons who select to build their faith on rock or sand. Perhaps a quiet waterfall might be included so that your altar would attract members during the weeks ahead, as a sacred spot for stopping to take a drink from the Fountain of Life, which never runs dry. Let your imagination flow and allow the artistry of your worship committee to make the garden one to remember. If you place lilies around the altar the day before Easter, the beauty will be striking!

This period of the church year also includes Women's History Month in March. International Women's History Day is March 8. You will find a focus on the contributions of women throughout the liturgies.

ASH WEDNESDAY

Joel 2:1–2, 12–17 or Isaiah 58:1–12
Psalm 51:1–17
2 Corinthians 5:20b–6:10
Matthew 6:1–6, 16–21

Call to Worship

(Read the Joel passage.)

(Have children dressed as clowns come in with garden implements and dirty hands. They are silent as they walk from the rear and smile at each row. They notice the cross at the altar and make attempts to kneel. But their dirty hands prevent them. One of the adult leaders, dressed as a clown, comes and offers to each child a sanitary premoistened wipe. They cleanse their hands and go kneel, signifying clean hearts before God. The children offer each of the congregation a premoistened wipe. A time of silent prayer is offered.)

Call to Confession

(Use the Psalm passage as a responsive confession. Allow time for silent confession.)

Words of Assurance

For our sake God made Jesus, who knew no sin, to be sin so that in him we might become the righteousness of God. . . . See, now is the acceptable time, with our confession. Now is the day of salvation. This is mighty good news.

Reading of the Gospel

Imposition of Ashes

(The palm branches of the preceding Palm Sunday will have been burned to become the necessary ashes. If they are not handy, a local florist or Catholic bookstore will have them available for purchase. Ash Wednesday is an occasion to remember our mortality and help us prepare for the six-week journey to the Resurrection Event that is to come and mark us with eternal life!)

Offertory Invitation

We will not put any obstacle in anyone's way, so that no fault may be found with our ministry, but as servants of God we have commended ourselves in every way. We give in order that others may come and experience new life in Christ.

Offertory Praise

God of all, your love towards us is so marvelous. We thank you for all you have given us. We rejoice in this opportunity to be poor enough in spirit that we gladly share to make others part of your realm. We give because we recognize that we have nothing of ourselves, but with your great love for us we possess everything!

Benediction

Leader: The journey to Calvary begins.
People: We commend ourselves to God.
Leader: The journey calls us to receive the grace of God for every facet of our lives.
People: We commend ourselves to God.
Leader: The journey will call for great endurance on our part.
People: We commend ourselves to God.
Leader: Take the journey enfolded by Love, Truth, and Power. I commend us to God.
People: Hallelujah and amen!

FIRST SUNDAY OF LENT

Deuteronomy 26:1–11
Psalm 91:1–2, 9–16,
Romans 10:8b–13
Luke 4:1–13

Call to Worship

Leader: This day marks the paradox of life!
People: In order to live fully, first we must die!
Leader: The Word is near you, on your lips and in your hearts.
People: If we confess with our lips that Jesus is Lord and believe in our hearts that God raised him from the dead, we will be saved!
Leader: For we believe with our heart and we are justified.
People: With the confession of our lips we are saved! For this reason, we gather to offer thanks and worship to the God of our salvation.

Call to Confession

Jesus, while full of the Holy Spirit, was led by the Spirit into the wilderness, where for forty days he was tempted by the devil. He did not sin. As we prepare for our forty-day Lenten journey, let us seek God for what we have already done. Shall we pray?

Confession

Director of our path, we have failed to follow you. Often your way leads to the wilderness and we prefer the lush green of the byways. We have not done what you have commanded. We have done all the things you told us not to do. Forgive us of our sin. Lead us into the paths of right living and help us have a willing desire to follow where your Holy Spirit leads. We pray in the name of the One who was victorious over the wilderness journey.

Words of Assurance

The Lord God is generous to all who call in faith, for "everyone who calls upon the name of the Lord shall be saved"! This is our confidence. It is good news.

Responsive Reading

Leader: A nameless group of stolen Africans are our ancestors.

People: They traveled the Middle Passage and many of them leaped to their deaths rather than survive as slaves in a foreign land.

Leader: Many of them died en route due to the horrible conditions on ships, where they were hauled as freight.

People: As aliens, in foreign soil, they became a great nation, mighty and many.

Leader: The least ones of them were strong enough to survive and begin to thrive.

People: They brought with them a trust, a hope, and a confidence in the High God.

Leader: In afflictions, toil, and oppression they cried out to God for deliverance and for freedom.

People: It was God who won for us the victory. With a mighty outstretched arm, with great displays of power, with signs and with wonders, God gave us emancipation. It was not Lincoln. It was not the Civil War. It was not the abolitionists. It was God.

Leader: We were sold by our own relatives into the hands of heathens who had our destruction in mind.

People: But God! God has brought us thus far along the way. We now live in houses we have not built. We eat from gardens that we do not plant. And we have the opportunities toward which our foreparents only dreamed. We are the hope and the dream of former slaves!

Offertory Invitation

Today, I declare to God that we have come into the land that God has ordained for us. We owe God a proper return of all that we have been provided. For, in the final analysis, it all belongs to God. Yet we can celebrate by sharing the bounty that the Lord our God has given us and our households.

Offertory Praise

We who live in the shelter of the Most High, we who abide in the shadow of the Almighty, say to thee, O God, that you are our refuge and our fortress. You are the God in whom we trust. You are our dwelling place and it is you that has kept evil from befalling us. You have given your angels to guard over us in all our ways. These gifts we offer as sacrificial praise in the name of Jesus Christ.

Benediction

Leader: Be love as you return to the world during Lent.
People: We will be love in our going out.
Leader: Be love as you return to the world during Lent.
People: We will be love in our coming in.
Leader: Be love as you return to the world during Lent.
People: We will be love in our leisure and at our work.
Leader: You are God's beloved children! Claim that power. Walk in that name!
People: Hallelujah and amen!

SECOND SUNDAY OF LENT

Genesis 15:1–12, 17–18
Psalm 27
Philippians 3:17–4:1
Luke 13:31–35 or 9:28–36

Call to Worship

Leader: The Covenant-Making God demands an audience with us.
People: Covenants are made between two with equal power. We have nothing to offer God.
Leader: The covenant is ours because of God's love for us.
People: God called Abram, made covenant with him, and sent Jesus as the Sacrificial Lamb.
Leader: The covenant is a legal and binding event, for God won't take it back.
People: The covenant involved people, land, and laws of right living.
Leader: The covenant established a lasting relationship between God and us.
People: Praise to the Covenant-Keeping God, who deserves our faithful worship.

Call to Confession

Our citizenship is in heaven, and it is from there that we are expecting a Savior. He will transform the body of our humiliation, that it may be conformed to the body of his glory. Because that day is coming soon and we want to be ready, let us offer prayers of confession.

Confession

Teach us your ways, O God, and lead us on a level path. Do not give us up to the will of the adversary of our soul. We have sinned and deserve death. Forgive us, we pray. Do not turn us away in anger, because you have been our constant help. Do not cast us off and forsake us. For you are the God of our salvation. Hear our prayer in the name of the Coming One.

Words of Assurance

I believe that we shall see the goodness of God in the land of the living. Therefore, my brothers and my sisters, wait for God; be strong. Let your heart take courage. Blessed is the one who comes in the name of the Lord. This is good news.

Responsive Reading

Leader: We can chill with God on our side. With the Light of God and the salvation of Jesus Christ, what is there to fear?

People: Fear may knock on our door, but faith always answers!

Leader: God has our back on every side. The ancestors called God a "leaning post."

People: Many are those who have tried to dis' us, rip us off, destroy our name, and even kill us.

Leader: Armies of evildoers have plotted, planned, and drawn up schemes for our demise. But God . . .

People: God cannot be figured out. God is the great mystery. God is everywhere at the same time.

Leader: God blows traps before we know anything about them. God kicks tail, but does not stop to take down names! When we look around, we have victory after victory and don't know how they actually came about.

People: We are confident of this one thing—God loves us and has been our help for generations. All that we require is a place to meet where we can talk about the goodness of our God.

Leader: Contemplate the mercies of God. Study the Word of God. Quiet your heart and listen to discern God in all that is around you.

People: In the midst of the anxious and noisy world, we go inward and tap into the stillness of our spirit. It makes no difference where we might be, for there is no spot where God is not!

Offertory Invitation

The covenant promised that God would be our shield and that our reward would be great. Great rewards demand great returns. For what we have belongs to God. We cannot beat God's giving, no matter how we try. Giving is an expression of our gratitude.

Offertory Praise

Prosperity, stability, and security are ours because of the covenant you made generations ago, God. We thank you for being a promise keeper. We celebrate your care by giving back a portion of what you have given us. We pray that these offerings will bring forth more spiritual fruit in your realm. Please accept them in the name of Jesus Christ.

Benediction

Leader: Leave this place with the power and conviction of being agents of healing.

People: We leave to journey into all the parts of this community with healing in our touch.

Leader: Leave this place with the power to make a difference in the world.

People: We leave to walk the talk of Jesus Christ and proclaim that salvation is here.

Leader: Leave this place with the creativity, the redemption, and the ability to make changes in the world. Go in peace. Love God, yourself, and your neighbors in all that you do.

People: Hallelujah and amen!

THIRD SUNDAY OF LENT

Isaiah 55:1–9
Psalm 63:1–8
1 Corinthians 10:1–13
Luke 13:1–9

Call to Worship

Leader: We come to give thanks to the God of another chance.
People: Thank God for the ability to start over again.
Leader: Last week's journey was not all we hoped it might be.
People: We left this place with good intentions, but life met us and often we failed.
Leader: Every failure is welcome in this place. Without price we will receive pardon and grace.
People: We relinquish our self-reliant ways and offer our worship to the God who keeps covenant with us despite ourselves. O come let us adore him, Christ the Lord.

Call to Confession

Seek the Lord, who may be found here. Call upon the Savior, who is near. Let the wicked forsake their ways, and the unrighteous their thoughts. With confession and repentance, let us return to God, who longs to have mercy upon us and to abundantly pardon our sin. Let us pray.

Confession

Creator God, my soul thirsts for you; my flesh faints for you as one in a dry and weary land where there is no water. We have tried to make it on our own this past week and have failed miserably. We know that your steadfast love is better than life, so we come and ask you to forgive the sin in us. We lift our hands in surrender and offer repentance. Hear us, we pray, in the name of Amazing Grace.

Words of Assurance

God is faithful and will not allow us to be tested beyond our strength. With every test God will provide for us the way out so that we may be able to endure it. This is good news. Thanks be to our forgiving God.

Responsive Reading

Leader: Like a dry shrub in the middle of the desert, so thirst our souls for the Living Water.
People: Like the parched land that yearns for drops of fresh rain, so our earthly flesh requires the Well of Life.
Leader: In the sanctuary we behold the memories of the God, who satisfies every longing.
People: We listen with attentive ears and drink in the collective memory of a satisfying Savior.
Leader: Our journey through the wilderness of life often leads us into those places where it is difficult to be refreshed with the things of God.
People: We have a hunger and a thirst that has not been touched with the things we have tried.
Leader: We gather to rehearse the stories. We come together to be reminded that God does not change.
People: There is water for the thirsty. There is bread for the hungry. The journey continues. And God will satisfy our needs.
Leader: We will lift our hands in this sanctuary.
People: We will bless the name of God. We will call upon the Name Above All Names.
Leader: God's commandments are not simple wishes. They save our lives.

Offertory Invitation

Everyone who is thirsty is invited to the waters; and you who have no money are invited to come, buy, and eat! Come buy wine and milk without money and without price? The invitation is given to all of the world. It is given because of the generosity of God, who anticipates our sharing to keep the way open for all who do not have. It is giving time.

Offertory Praise

God of the Harvest, we are the fig tree that you have allowed to stand in places where we were not to grow, bloom, or thrive. Yet your grace has kept us and offers us another chance to be part of your sowing and reaping cycle. Accept these gifts that we offer in the name of our Help and our Hope, Jesus the Christ.

Benediction

Leader: Leave to be fig trees that bloom and blossom in the hard places of Lent.

People: We go in the name of the Owner of the Vineyard.

Leader: Leave with the understanding that you will be tempted and tried.

People: We go in the faith that the One who plants us will tend to our every need.

Leader: Leave to be the symbols of fruitfulness that the world needs to experience.

People: We go with full knowledge that we must grow and be fruitful or die.

Leader: God the Owner, Jesus the Chief Gardener, and the Tending Holy Spirit will keep us on our way.

People: Hallelujah and amen.

FOURTH SUNDAY OF LENT

Joshua 5:9–12
Psalm 32
2 Corinthians 5:16–21
Luke 15:1–3, 11b–32

Call to Worship

Leader: The God of Instruction calls us together.
People: We gather with teachable spirits.
Leader: The God Who Counsels has words of wisdom to provide.
People: We have come to be directed toward better and more abundant living.
Leader: The God of New Beginnings is available.
People: We assemble with various needs of fresh starts. We come to the God of New Life.

Call to Confession

Happy are those people whose transgressions are forgiven and whose sin is covered. Happy are those people to whom God charges no hidden sins and in whom God finds no deceit. The world says "Don't worry. Be happy." We know that happiness for the people of God comes from our confession. Let us pray.

Confession

God, as we try to keep silent about our inner state of being, our bodies waste away through our groans and sighs all the day and night long. Our strength is dried up, like the hot days of summer. So we come to acknowledge our sin to you and to stop trying to hide from you all the many things we have done that separate us from your love. Forgive us. We confess our guilt and sin. We pray in the name of our Salvation.

Words of Assurance

God is our hiding place and a preserver from trouble. God is our teacher, who instructs us in the way to life eternal. Many are the torments of the wicked, but steadfast love surrounds those of us whose trust is in God. Sisters and brothers, this is good news. Thanks be unto God.

Responsive Reading

Leader: It's time to make noise in here! The love of God has sustained us another week.

People: It's time for us to raise the roof with our thanksgiving. For God has been mighty good.

Leader: Let the redeemed of the Lord say so! If you have been delivered from troubles this week, give out a shout.

People: Praise God!

Leader: Fresh starts, new beginnings, and brand new pages are recorded in the Book of Life as we are lovingly forgiven and restored by God.

People: We are blessed of God, indeed.

Leader: Trying to hide our foolishness from God simply does not work. The inner turmoil betrays the smiling face that we try to show the world.

People: Most of our physical ailments are the signs of our inner distresses.

Leader: Since God already knows the things we think and do before we think and do them, it's foolish not to confess, repent, and allow God to rip out the bad page and give us a new slate.

People: It's a joy to know that the accounting of God justifies our accounts with our confessions.

Leader: When we come clean with ourselves and with God, the pressure is released, the fears disappear, and the hope seems to return to our lives.

People: God knows us intimately. We are foolish to not be honest with ourselves when life begins to turn sour on us. God is our getaway place. God longs to be in relationship with us. God is displeased when we play games of hide and seek. We lift our hands in this sanctuary for our forgiving and reconciling God. Bless God, O my soul.

Offertory Invitation

We are ambassadors for Christ! This is a strong statement that calls us to do for the world, in the name of Jesus Christ, those greater works left to our hands. Giving helps us to entrust the message of reconciliation to the world. Freely we have received. Freely let us share in the offering.

Offertory Praise

For our sakes, God, you made Jesus to be sin, who knew no sin. Through his atoning work at Calvary we have been made new creatures in Christ. All we have to offer in repayment is our lives and what we do with them. Please accept these tokens of praise for our new life. In the name of the Giver of Life, we pray.

Benediction

Leader: Prodigal sons and daughters, we leave to continue the journey of Lent.

People: For all our wasteful and riotous living, we have been welcomed home.

Leader: We are not worthy to be called by the name of a gracious Parent who receives us with such love.

People: We leave to live out our gratitude by calling other prodigal children to God this week.

Leader: God the Great Parent, Jesus Christ the Calling-Home Son, and the Welcoming Holy Spirit, the Power, will keep us as we return to the season of Lent. Go in peace and power.

People: Hallelujah and amen.

FIFTH SUNDAY OF LENT

Isaiah 43:16–21
Psalm 126
Philippians 3:4b–14
John 12:1–8

Call to Worship

Leader: The God of extravagant love demands our attention.
People: God has done great things for us in the past week; we gather as living testimonies.
Leader: The journey to Calvary is our story to rehearse.
People: God's Only Begotten Son was born to die for our sin.
Leader: The journey to Lent is our death to self and our arising to new life in Christ.
People: We long to worship Christ, who calls us to rise from every situation with hope. Let our praise anoint him this day.

Call to Confession

We profess that we want to know Christ and the power of his resurrection and the sharing of his sufferings by becoming like him in his death through our baptism. Yet our lives prove different. For the journey to Lent has shown that we don't like to suffer. And surely we don't want our flesh to die. Our talk has not been our way. It's time for confession.

Confession

God, you have done great things for us and we have rejoiced. God, you have demanded great things from us and we have failed you. Restore us. Forgive our sin. Let us drink from the Well that never runs dry. Hear our prayers, through Christ we pray.

Words of Assurance

Those who go out with weeping, bearing the seed for sowing, shall come home with shouts of joy, carrying their sheaves from God's harvest. This is our good news!

Responsive Reading

Leader: Good God, it seems too good to be true.

People: Sometimes we are afraid that we will awake from a dream.

Leader: Our good fortune despite our beginnings in this nation is overwhelming.

People: Truly, we have moved a mighty long ways.

Leader: The talk against us has been legendary.

People: The plots against us have been too numerous to count. Yet God has been merciful to us.

Leader: God's wonders are new and fresh every morning.

People: We have a heritage from God instead of the horrors that were to be our destiny.

Leader: The tearful petitions that we have raised are enough to be everlasting waterfalls.

People: God has stored them on our account and sends refreshing rains upon our lives.

Leader: We don't live in a drought condition, for we serve the Master Gardener.

People: Our tears only last for a short season when compared to the joy that God brings our way. God has given us a harvest of laughter. The journey continues and we are refreshed.

Offertory Invitation

The more we come to know the movement of Christ in our lives, the more we become like the Apostle Paul, who said, "Whatever gains I had, these I have come to regard as loss because of the surpassing value of knowing Christ Jesus my Lord." This is encouraging as we prepare our hearts to share in the offering.

Offertory Praise

God, it is not that we have already obtained or reached our goal, but we press on to make your goal for our lives a reality, because Jesus has made us his own. For this reason we give to the One who first loved us. It's in the name of the Christ that we pray.

Benediction

Leader: This is the day when a godly woman anointed Jesus as King.

People: We leave to touch the world.

Leader: The crowd of men were not impressed with her offering.

People: What we have to give might not be impressive either. But we will reach out to make a difference in the world this week.

Leader: Go in the power of the Touching God, the Receiving Christ, and the Holy Companion. Like Mary, change the world with what you have to offer. Jesus has already told them to leave you alone. Go in peace and power.

People: It is so!

PALM SUNDAY

Isaiah 50:4–9a
Psalm 118:1–2, 19–29
Philippians 2:5–11
Luke 19:28–40

Call to Worship

Leader: Let this mind be in us that was also in Christ Jesus, who, though he was in the form of God, did not regard equality with God as something to be exploited.

People: But Jesus emptied himself, taking on the form of a slave, being born in human likeness and being found in human form. He humbled himself and became obedient to the point of death—even death on a cross.

Leader: Therefore God has also highly exalted Jesus and has given him a name that is above every name.

People: At the name of Jesus every knee should bow, in heaven and on earth and under the earth, and every tongue should confess that Jesus Christ is Lord to the glory of God. For this cause we have gathered to worship and proclaim his worthy name.

Call to Confession

Jesus looked at his disciples the night of his betrayal and declared, "But see, the one who betrays me is with me." So all who gather in that holy name will not meet him face to face in peace. Our confession clears the way from the many times we have betrayed him. Shall we pray?

Confession

God, like the disciples we have eaten at your table and declared we would remember Jesus. Then, like the disciples we have left this sacred space and gone into the world and betrayed our Savior. We have slept when we should have prayed. We have fought when we were needed to be peacemakers. Surely, we have been the betrayers. Forgive our sin. Restore our relationship, we pray, in the name of the One who called "Remember me."

Words of Assurance

God has given us the tongues of teachers so that we would know how to sustain the weary with our words. Morning by morning we awaken with ears to listen as those who are taught. With confession we are not in rebellion. The Sovereign helps us, restores us, and keeps us from being disgraced. This is our good news.

Responsive Reading

Leader: We have walked with Jesus during Lent. It is the time of transition.
People: What can we do? What do we have to bring?
Leader: Jesus sent the disciples to get an animal and told the owner, "The Lord needs it." That was enough.
People: What can we do? What do we have to bring?
Leader: The Maker of heaven and earth, of animal and humankind, had to borrow something for the Palm Sunday parade.
People: What can we do? What do we have to bring?
Leader: It's time to move into Holy Week. The world will be watching for Jesus to die again.
People: What can we do? What do we have to bring?
Leader: Jesus needs to borrow your eyes to see the hurting everywhere.
People: What can we do? What do we have to bring?
Leader: Jesus needs to borrow your hands to lift up the downtrodden.
People: What can we do? What do we have to bring?
Leader: Jesus needs to borrow your feet to carry the message of resurrection to the world.
People: What can we do? What do we have to bring?
Leader: Jesus needs to borrow your tongues to hold fast to the words of life and not get quiet after the parade.
People: What can we do? What do we have to bring?
Leader: The Maker of All needs to use you. Untie all that you have bound within you and let's get busy this week for the realm of God.
People: What we are we offer freely. We bring ourselves and will walk the talk of Easter people. We will fall down. But the amazing grace of the Christ will pick us up again. This is our story and this is our theme of praise.

Offertory Invitation

Jesus shared a sacred meal of bread and wine with his friends. It was a common meal that represented family and community. The need for family and community continues around the world. What we share today extends the family ties. Let's be generous in our giving.

Offertory Praise

God, we trust in you and declare before the world that you are our God. Our times are in your hands as you deliver us from the hands of every enemy. As we have shared our resources we ask that your face continue to shine upon us and save us in your steadfast love, we pray in the name of our Servant and your Son.

Benediction

Leader: May God be gracious unto us this week, for distress and grief are loose in the world.

People: Our lives are spent with sorrow, our years with sighing; our strength fails because of misery, and even our bones waste away as we are the scorn of our adversaries. Yet we follow the Christ.

Leader: May God be gracious unto us this week, for Jesus will become for us the broken vessel. We are called to do the same.

People: Satan has demanded to sift us like wheat, but Jesus has prayed for us that our faith may not fail, and when we have turned back, we are to strengthen others on the journey to Calvary.

Leader: Pray that you may not come to the time of trial. And when you do, know that the Victory, the Amen, and the Power go before us.

People: Hallelujah and amen.

HOLY WEEK

The ageless story is played out again during Holy Week. The I Am walks the human experience that ends in death. The pain, the hurt, the rejection, and the anointing that send Jesus forth are all part of the drama of the last seven days of the human existence of the Christ. This God-man who entered history at Bethlehem exits at an old rugged cross on a garbage dump outside Jerusalem. From royalty to rejection, from innocence to evil, and from infant to infamous we walk the dusty streets with Jesus and his followers. The story never grows old.

Instead of using the Psalms as a responsive reading, I have provided a litany based upon the travels of Jesus. It may be helpful to provide a few moments of silence for personal reflection and meditation following the readings.

This period of walking with Jesus to Calvary is one to engage those not usually involved in the "busy life" of the congregation. Pulling together men and women who are retired to prepare the soup and salad each day gives ample opportunity for community building. Another suggestion would be to have this type of worship during each week of Lent. You may be pleasantly surprised at who will show up to a noon worship experience. Offering plates should be placed at the rear of the sanctuary and simply mentioned after the benediction. What monies are received will offset the cost of food and kitchen supplies. A particular mission in your local community can become the focus of any additional funds received.

Target schools, businesses, doctors' offices, and the area within a six-block radius of your building to leave flyers announcing lunch and meditation with a "free will offering." If your mission's work area is already involved with a local outreach project, mention it in your publicity. Some people who attend no congregation will be glad to give to "charity." Your church gets the credit and earns "brownie points" for caring. Invite those who "brown bag" for lunch to come and share the worship time with others as we journey to Calvary. Make this a meaningful occasion for Christ to touch hearts!

MONDAY OF HOLY WEEK

Isaiah 42:1–9
Psalm 36:5–11
Hebrews 9:11–15
John 12:1–11

Call to Worship

Leader: Here is God's servant, whom we uphold, God's chosen, in whom our soul delights.
People: God's spirit is upon him. Jesus will bring forth justice to the nations.
Leader: He will not cry or lift up his voice or make it heard in the street.
People: A bruised reed he will not break, and a dimly burning wick he will not quench.
Leader: Jesus will not grow faint or be crushed.
People: He is preparing to establish justice in the earth. We walk with him this week.

Call to Confession

The steadfast love of our God extends to the heavens. God's faithfulness is beyond the clouds. Our confession allows us the ability to take refuge in the shadow of God's wings. Let us pray.

Confession

The blood of goats and heifers will not satisfy the sacrifice required for us. We thank you, God, for the blood of Jesus Christ, who entered once for all into the Holy Place. Forgive us our sin. In the name of Love, we pray. Amen.

Responsive Reading

Leader: Monday is the day of Jesus Christ's anointing.
People: The grateful dead was present.
Leader: Lazarus had already experienced resurrection.
People: The ungrateful thief was present.

Leader: Judas had his eye on what could be stolen.

People: Jesus was present.

Leader: And a woman anointed him as King.

People: She poured the anointing oil on his head as on a high priest.

Leader: She knelt down and worshiped at his feet.

People: The fragrance of her expensive ointment filled the room.

Leader: Instead of using the ointment for her own burial, she poured it all on Jesus.

People: Her anointing prepared Jesus for the cross that was ahead.

Leader: The poor were present. They are yet among us. Jesus noticed them.

People: A great crowd was present watching the sights, but not worshiping.

Leader: We gather to worship. We will walk with Jesus during this week of holy days.

Silent meditation and personal reflection

Benediction

Leader: Christ is the mediator of a new covenant.

People: We have been called to a new inheritance because of the sacrifice of Jesus.

Leader: Go in peace! Amen.

TUESDAY OF HOLY WEEK

Isaiah 49:1–7
Psalm 71:1–14
1 Corinthians 1:18–31
John 12:20–36

Call to Worship

Leader: Why have you gathered?
People: We want to see Jesus!
Leader: The Light is with us for only a little longer.
People: We will walk in the light.

Call to Confession

On this second day of Holy Week, as we walk toward Calvary, let us confess before God.

Confession

Loving God, the message of the cross is foolishness to those who are perishing, but to us who are being saved it is the power of God. Forgive us our sin. Fill us with the power to follow you.

Words of Assurance

God is never far from us. The words of our confession draw us closer to the heart of God. This is good news.

Responsive Reading

Leader: The hour is coming closer. The appointed time is near.
People: Unless a grain of wheat falls to the earth and dies, it remains just a single grain.
Leader: But if it dies, it bears much fruit.
People: Those who love their life lose it. And those who hate their life in this world will keep it for eternal life.

Leader: Whoever serves Jesus must follow. For where Jesus goes, we must go also.

People: Now my soul is troubled! And what should we say?

Leader: It was for this reason that Jesus was born to die.

People: God will get the glory.

Leader: And the world will be judged.

People: The ruler of this world will be driven out.

Leader: And Jesus will be lifted up for all the world to see.

People: We walk with Jesus to Calvary.

Silent meditation and personal reflection

Benediction

Leader: If you walk in the darkness you do not know where you are going.

People: We leave to walk in the light. We are children of light.

Leader: The Light is with you a little longer. Go in peace!

WEDNESDAY OF HOLY WEEK

Isaiah 50:4–9a
Psalm 70
Hebrews 12:1–3
John 13:21–32

Call to Worship

Leader: God has given us tongues that we might teach others.
People: God calls us to sustain the weary with our meager words.
Leader: Morning by morning God gives us alert ears.
People: God has opened our ears so we may be taught.
Leader: When we do not rebel and turn from God, we will be used in ministry to the world.
People: Let us stand up together. The Sovereign God is our constant help.

Call to Confession

God is pleased to deliver us. We only need to ask forgiveness for our sin.

Confession

Gracious God, we have been rebellious and turned away from you. We have fallen into sin and brought disgrace to our witness. Forgive us our sin. Deliver us. Set our face like flint so that we might see no evil, hear no evil, and do no evil in your sight. Declare us "not guilty" in order that we may serve you in the world.

Words of Assurance

Therefore, since we are surrounded by so great a cloud of witnesses, let us also lay aside every weight and the sin that clings so closely, and let us run with perseverance the race that is set before us, looking to Jesus, the pioneer and perfecter of our faith, who for the sake of the joy that was set before him endured the cross, disregarding its shame, and has taken his seat at the right hand of the throne of God. Consider him who endured such hostility against himself from sinners, so that you may not grow weary or lose heart. My sisters and brothers, this is certainly good news!

Responsive Reading

Leader: The Teacher became a mother one night.
People: Jesus prepared his children a meal. He used his own body and his own blood.
Leader: The Great One became a mother one night.
People: Jesus prepared his children a bath and washed their dirty feet.
Leader: The Parent became sad one night.
People: After preparing and serving, washing and wishing, he knew betrayal was close at hand.
Leader: Jesus said, "Very truly, I tell you, one of you will betray me."
People: John asked, "Lord, who is it?"
Leader: That question continues to ring loud among us today.
People: We ask, "Lord, is it me?"

Silent meditation and personal reflection

Benediction

Leader: We are walking with Jesus to Calvary.
People: Who among us will betray the Sovereign of Creation?
Leader: Go in peace!

HOLY THURSDAY

In the black Church, this night has been deemed appropriate for the washing of feet. It is an old custom that seems to have lost its appeal in recent generations. Yet the Savior washed the feet of his disciples on this sacred night. And we can return to this tradition, which indicates humility and service to another. If feet washing is not desired, some sort of hand washing ritual may be exchanged, with lotion provided to conclude our act of care. It is also the night that the Passover Meal is celebrated. This meal is the one eaten just before the children of Israel began their exodus from slavery in Egypt. As they were to be busy packing up and preparing for the signal to move out, the meal was to be eaten while the participants were on alert. On this night, Holy Thursday, the congregation could be asked to pack the typical meal that our ancestors might have packed as they were preparing for moving out under the cover of night for freedom. Brought in picnic baskets, this meal is a prime opportunity to celebrate together and to covenant anew to be community for each other.

Call to Worship
(Read Exodus 12:1–14.)

Song of Celebration

Call to Sharing a Meal

The feast of the slave community has always held a special place in our hearts. We can easily remember Granny packing the basket as we made ready to travel to worship, to a quilting bee, or simply to spend time with our kin. As we migrated from the South to the North and Midwest, we can recall with fondness the many brown bags packed with fried chicken, homemade rolls, deviled eggs, fried pies, and potato salad that traveled with us in trains, buses, and cars. These meals sustained us in times that the dining cars didn't welcome us. Eating together has been part of our salvation. The Jewish community has its meal, which Jesus celebrated with his friends. In that same spirit, tonight we will open our picnic baskets around the tables and share with our friends. Freedom is on the way. Let's be ready to heed its call.

Table Grace

God, you continue to call us to make haste for freedom. We thank you for your call. As we gather around these tables in celebration of the awesome ministry of Jesus to and with his friends, help us to remember his servant attitude. He prepared and served a meal. He washed the feet of his friends and affirmed them. Help us to follow his example on this holy night. Bless the abundance of food that has been prepared and that we will eat. Bless each hand that touched it in order that it grace our tables. Bless those folks with little and those with none tonight. Bless those folks who are yet willingly shackled in bondage. Sanctify this food as nourishment for our bodies. And when we leave this place, let its nutrition energize us enough to work towards the day when the world can gather around banquet tables like these with thanksgiving. In the name of Jesus Christ we pray. Amen.

After-supper Response

Congregational song of praise

Scripture Reading

(John 13:1–7, 31b–35)

Invitation to Servanthood

Love is an action verb. Our foreparents washed each others' feet as a sign of love, care, and service. Tonight we will offer a similar sign by washing each others' hands. Handiwipes are available at each table. After each one has cleaned another's hand, let us take the time to put lotion on that same pair of hands. Then let us pray for the ministry opportunities before our neighbors.

Hymn of Praise

Call to Communion

(Read 1 Corinthians 11:23–26. Communion is served.)

Benediction

(Read responsively Psalm 116:1–2, 12–19.)
Leader: Go in peace to love God and to serve your neighbors in all that you do.
People: Amen and amen.

GOOD FRIDAY

This worship experience is an alternative to the preaching style commonly used. This can be a worship of scripture and songs appropriate to the Word Jesus speaks. It is a time when lay speakers, young and senior, can participate in meaningful ways.

The sanctuary is dark as the congregation gathers. Acolytes enter and light altar candles. The processional of the choir is next, followed by the a capella singing of an appropriate spiritual. When they are finished and seated, the spotlight follows Jesus and Simon, slowly coming up the aisle bearing the cross. It is laid against pulpit where it is very visible. Liturgical dancers become the women at the Cross as we hear the pounding of the nails in the distance.

Call to Worship

(Isaiah 52:13–53:12)

(Jesus, Simon, and liturgical dancers leave as congregation stands to sing music selected by musicians)

Invocation

On this most sacred night we gather to remember. We remember the greatest sacrifice of love. We remember the journey of Jesus to the cross. We remember the price Jesus paid for our salvation. We remember the women whom Jesus told not to cry for him, but to cry for themselves and their children. We remember that all of his disciples but one ran away, afraid. We remember that Jesus was left with three women and one man as they crucified him for our sin. And we remember our sinful nature that nailed him to the cross, alone. Tonight we gather to be present. Shall we pray?

Gracious God, this night we gather to remember. Thank you for Jesus. Thank you for your presence. Thank you for your love. Thank you for this holy memory. For the sake of Jesus Christ, we pray. Amen.

Scripture

(Hebrews 10:16–25)

Congregational Hymn

Seven Last Words of Jesus: The First Word
(Luke 23:26–38) *Father Forgive Them*

Solo

Seven Last Words of Jesus: The Second Word
(Luke 23:39–43) *Today You Are with Me*

Congregational Hymn

Seven Last Words of Jesus: The Third Word
(John 19:25–27) *Woman, Behold Thy Son*

The Liturgical Dancers

Seven Last Words of Jesus: The Fourth Word
(John 19:28) *I Thirst*

Congregational Hymn

Seven Last Words of Jesus: The Fifth Word
(Psalm 22) *My God, My God, Why?*

Solo

Seven Last Words of Jesus: The Sixth Word
(Luke 23:44–46) *Into Thy Hands*

The Male Chorus

Seven Last Words of Jesus: The Seventh Word
(John 19:29–30) *It Is Finished!*

(The pastor invites all musical participants and dancers to the altar. Each one is given a nail for the cross. Sound effects, offstage, enlarge the sound of pounding.

The pastor invites the congregation to the altar as ushers hand out nails for taking home to remember this significant night. The congregation can bring their offerings forward as they come to kneel and pray. When the last person leaves the altar, the music ceases.

When all have finished, in silence the communion stewards strip the altar. The lights are turned off with the exception of a spotlight on the cross. There is a space of silence. The pastor instructs the congregation to leave in thanksgiving and silence. There is no additional music or talking.)

HOLY SATURDAY

Call to Worship

Leader: Each of us is born.
People: Our days are too short and filled with trouble.
Leader: We come up like a flower and we wither.
People: Like a fleeting shadow we do not last.
Leader: Our days are determined.
People: Our death is certain.
Leader: Yesterday, death claimed Jesus!
People: A funeral procession followed his body to a borrowed tomb.
Leader: It is not the end of the story.
People: Thanks be to God.

Call to Confession

Mortals die. Jesus died. He was ready, prepared, and able to say, "It is finished!" Our confession helps us to stay prepared to meet death. Let us pray.

Confession

In you, O God, we seek refuge; do not let us ever be put to shame. Forgive our sin. In your righteousness, deliver us from the bonds of death. Incline your ears to us. Rescue us speedily. Be our rock of refuge and our strong fortress of salvation. Our times are in your hand. In the name of the Savior, we pray.

Words of Assurance

God's face shines upon us when we confess our sin. It is with steadfast love that we are forgiven and made whole. This is good news.

Responsive Reading

Leader: A wealthy but secret disciple, Joseph of Arimathea, received the body of Jesus for burial.

People: Lord, where were your vocal followers?
Leader: Pilate allowed a secret disciple to take the wrapped body of a dead Jesus and lay it in a borrowed tomb.
People: Lord, where were your vocal followers?
Leader: A great stone was rolled in front of the door to seal the tomb. The funeral procession was very small. There were three women and one man, a disciple, at the funeral.
People: Lord, where were your vocal followers?
Leader: The chief priests and the Pharisees gathered before Pilate to plot.
People: Lord, where were your vocal followers?
Leader: They decided to put guards all around the tomb to keep Jesus locked inside a grave.
People: Lord, where were your vocal followers?
Leader: The women followers sat silent, opposite the tomb, preparing to do their last act of loving ministry to a dead corpse at the proper time.
People: Jesus died. His followers did not remember his words of assurance that he would rise. Today the whole world waits as Jesus lies in a tomb.
Leader: Lord, where are your vocal followers?

Silence

Benediction

Leader: Go into the world! Be a vocal disciple. Tell the world that resurrection will raise the dead! Tell it everywhere you go!
People: Hallelujah and amen!

5 · THE EASTER SEASON

The resurrection is about our ability to rise! Jesus was tormented, mocked, publicly shamed, and ultimately killed. Evil felt it had the final word. Death considered itself a victor. The grave thought itself "the end." But Jesus got up! Evil's chain was broken. Death's hold was denied. The grave was forced to release its captive. God's power was evidenced as Jesus, the Christ, rose from the grave.

The resurrection is about our ability to be like Jesus Christ and to rise! We rise above evil circumstances. We rise above the death of hopes and dreams. We rise above our graves of depression, desolation, and despair. Every Sunday worship experience is another celebration of the resurrection. Getting up and beginning again is our theme song of joyous and unending praise.

EASTER SUNDAY

Acts 10:34–43 or Isaiah 65:17–25
Psalm 118:1–2, 14–24
1 Corinthians 15:19–26
John 20:1–18 or Luke 24:1–12

Call to Worship

Leader: Christ the Lord is risen!

People: Christ the Lord is risen indeed!

Leader: We celebrate the God who stood waiting for a lost woman in the Garden!

People: We celebrate the woman who stayed there, watching the tomb, looking for Jesus!

Leader: We honor the man who was mistaken for a gardener; he was the Risen Savior.

People: We remember the woman who was given the message to go and tell the resurrection story to her brothers.

Leader: Mary Magdalene became the second Eve. The old garden passed away.

People: New life begins again. Christ the Lord is risen indeed!

Call to Confession

Mary Magdalene went and announced to the disciples "I have seen the Lord." She told them what Jesus had said to them. They went seeking the Lord of Life. Our confession allows us their experience. Let us pray.

Confession

God, we are an Easter people and the resurrection story is our song of praise. We tend to fall down often. We tend to want to make a home in the graves of our lives. But you raised Jesus as our example of getting up, and today the story is reenacted in our lives. Forgive our sin. Pick us up. Let us experience a new beginning, we pray in the name of the One who rose victorious over sin, death, hell, and the grave.

Words of Assurance

Leader: The right hand of the Lord is exalted; the right hand of the Lord does valiant things for us.

People: We shall not die, but we shall live. And we will recount the mighty deeds of Jesus Christ, who has not given us over to death. The stone that the builders rejected has become the chief cornerstone. It is God's doing and it is marvelous in our eyes. This is the day that the Lord has made; we will rejoice and be glad in it!

Responsive Reading

Leader: God's strong love just won't quit!

People: Just when it seems that life has us at the point of no return . . .

Leader: God's strong love just won't quit!

People: Fridays and gloom keep on coming at us hard, but . . .

Leader: God's strong love just won't quit!

People: When we have been hemmed in on every side and need a refuge for our weary souls . . .

Leader: God's strong love just won't quit!

People: When it appears that evil has won and the victory belongs to Satan . . .

Leader: God's strong love just won't quit!

People: When the last nail seems to be pounding on the coffin of our dreams and hopes . . .

Leader: God's strong love just won't quit!

People: When, like Mary, we have walked the floor all night long and felt that death had won . . .

Leader: God's strong love just won't quit!

People: In the stillness of the midnight hour, we hear the One who knows us by name . . .

Leader: God's strong love just won't quit!

People: As Jesus was raised to new life, taking the sting from death and the victory from the grave . . .

Leader: God's strong love just won't quit!

People: The story is revisited in our lives over and over and over again, for . . .

Leader: God's strong love just won't quit! It's our job to tell the world that . . .

People: Our God's strong love just won't quit!

Offertory Invitation

God has tested us and pushed us hard during this Lenten season so that we might better appreciate this day of victorious celebration. In that spirit of a journey being over as a new one begins, let us share in the continuing story of resurrection.

Offertory Praise

God, in this house your name is Great. In these temples your praises are upon our lips. We have no right to sing the blues. For you are the One who has lifted our heads above the situations and circumstances that brought others death. We live, for Jesus lives. We give these offerings as a symbol of our love to the Risen Christ.

Benediction

Leader: Jesus Christ has been raised from the dead!
People: It was done that I might keep on getting up.
Leader: Jesus Christ gave Mary Magdalene a new message to carry.
People: It was a message just for me.
Leader: Jesus Christ has the victory over sin, death, and hell.
People: He did it just for me to have new life and life eternally.
Leader: He is risen!
People: Christ the Lord is risen indeed!
Leader: Go in that faith-filled power to love God and to serve your neighbor in all that you do!
People: Hallelujah and amen.

SECOND SUNDAY OF EASTER

Acts 5:27–32
Psalm 118:14–29 or 150
Revelation 1:4–8
John 20:19–31

Call to Worship

Leader: Grace to you and peace from Jesus Christ, who is and who was and who is to come!
People: We gather to worship Jesus Christ, the faithful witness, the first-born of the dead, and the ruler of all the earth.
Leader: To him who loves us and freed us from our sins by his blood, we owe great praise.
People: We are stormy-weather people, seeking the Son!
Leader: God has made us a realm of priests to serve this present age.
People: To the All Wise God and to Jesus Christ be glory and dominion forever and forever. Amen!

Call to Confession

We pledged allegiance to the Risen Savior last week and went out and did the same deeds that nailed him to the tree. In order to hold fast to our profession of faith we need confession to clear the way. Let's take this opportunity to pray together.

Confession

Self-Revealing One, we believed Mary's report of the resurrection. But we have been hidden away for so long, been afraid for so long, and been anxious for so long that freedom to live is scary! When we should have spoken up, we were quiet. When we had nothing to say, we spoke empty words that did not bless others. Forgive us the sin that separates us from you. Help us to love you, ourselves, and others, we pray in the name of the Risen Savior.

Words of Assurance

Leader: Jesus said to the hidden and scared disciples, "Peace be with you. As God has sent me, so I send you." Then he breathed on them and said to them, "Receive the Holy Spirit." The peace of Christ be with you.
People: And also with you. Amen.

Responsive Reading

Leader: Our strength, our might, our power, and our salvation are not our own.
People: The praise, the glory, the power, and the dominion belong to the strong hand of our God.
Leader: We lift high the name of the One who was, who is, and who is to come.
People: We celebrate the Mystery we dare to call the Trinity.
Leader: We have not died but rather we have been given new life.
People: We sing loud songs of victory, for God has done great things on our behalf.
Leader: We look forward to the times that we gather, for we give strength to each other with our testimonies of overcoming.
People: Thank God for the blood of Jesus that covers our sin and keeps us day by day.

Offertory Invitation

Blessed are we who have believed the report of a risen Christ. Through believing that Jesus is the Messiah, the Son of the Living God, we now have life in that powerful name. Until all come into this saving knowledge, the gift of sharing will continue. Let's give generously.

Offertory Praise

God, we must obey you rather than any human authority or worldly wisdom. The economy says to save—to keep and to invest for ourselves. Yet we believe the report of our ancestors who followed your way and gave their tithes so that we might have a place to gather and rehearse the old, old story of your amazing love. We pray that these, our gifts, keep the message going, for it's in the name of the Giver of New Life that we share.

Benediction

Leader: Peace be with you!
People: And peace be multiplied with you!

Leader: Receive the Holy Spirit!

People: Let it breathe upon us again!

Leader: The call of God, the shalom of Christ, and the peace of the Holy Spirit are ours!

People: Thanks be unto the God of Resurrection! Amen.

THIRD SUNDAY OF EASTER

Acts 9:1–20
Psalm 30
Revelation 5:11–14
John 21:1–19

Call to Worship

Leader: Then I looked and I heard the voice of many angels surrounding the throne.
People: There were living creatures, and the elders. They numbered myriads of myriads and thousands of thousands.
Leader: They sang a loud song of praise with full voice.
People: Worthy is the Lamb that was slain to receive power and wealth and wisdom and might and honor and glory and blessing!
Leader: Then I heard every creature in heaven and on earth and under the earth and in the sea, and all that was in them sang.
People: To the One seated on the throne and to the Lamb be blessing and honor and glory and might forever and ever. Amen.

Call to Confession

When Jesus showed up on the banks of the river and discovered that the disciples had returned to their former life, he asked them, "Children, do you have any meat?" Their answer was "No!" for they were caught doing the wrong thing with their lives. We have been caught. We have nothing to offer but our confession.

Confession

Here we are, God, caught with our childish ways. Here we are, God, looking silly. After all our strong words, we have been caught doing the same things we did before we accepted Christ. Forgive us our sin and feed us with the Bread of Life. We pray in the name of the Risen Christ.

Words of Assurance

The Savior has chosen us as instruments, chosen to bring the Name Above All Names before the world. With our confession, this is what can do. This is our good news!

Responsive Reading

Leader: God is sending us to the street called straight!
People: We have been dodging down the crooked ways, going through alleys and cutting corners on God.
Leader: God is sending us to the street called straight!
People: There are so many messes that we have made with our lives. We have tried to take the back roads and sometimes even the low roads, seeking shortcuts to salvation.
Leader: God is sending us to the street called straight!
People: We have lost our way. We have truly messed up. We have tried to walk with the world and to be politically correct.
Leader: God is sending us to the street called straight!
People: The old ways have dishonored God and gotten us into plenty of trouble.
Leader: God is sending us to the street called straight!
People: We will not be popular there. We won't have many friends.
Leader: God is sending us to the street called straight!
People: Easter does call us to acknowledge that we have turned from God's way and followed our own ways. The end of our way is death. Thank God for Jesus, who made it easy for us to take the street called straight! At the end of straight street we will find eternal life!

Offertory Invitation

Jesus' question to the disciples after the resurrection was "Do you have anything here to eat?" The disciples were caught off guard and the reality helped them to see Jesus more clearly. It is not in what we have that we see Jesus. It is in what we share that others see the reality of the Risen Christ. Let us give with a spirit of generosity.

Offertory Praise

Jesus fed the disciples with the fish they had caught after casting their nets on the right side. The right side is where Jesus instructs us to be. Giving is the right side of being blessed. God, we thank you for this opportunity in the name of the One who calls and feeds. Amen.

Benediction

Leader: The Messiah yet wants to know if we love him enough to feed his lambs.

People: Jesus knows that we love him.

Leader: The Savior yet wants to know if we love him enough to feed his sheep.

People: Jesus knows that we love him.

Leader: The Anointed One yet wants to know if we love him enough to tell a dying world about him.

People: Jesus knows that we love him, for he lives in us and shines forth in all that we do.

Leader: Leave to follow Jesus Christ, knowing that the Promise Keeper and the Power go before us.

People: Hallelujah and amen!

FOURTH SUNDAY OF EASTER

Acts 9:36–43
Psalm 23
Revelation 7:9–17
John 10:22–30

Call to Worship

Leader: We have come at the call of the Good Shepherd.
People: It's good to be in the number one more time.
Leader: The lost, the straying, the hurt, and the lame are invited to this fold.
People: It's good to be in the number one more time.
Leader: There is anointing oil and sweet grass available for every hungry sheep.
People: It is good to be in the number one more time. We come to feast, to be healed, and to offer praise.

Call to Confession

We have been the church on the go this week. Many of us forgot the roles we were to play and forgot to whose fold we belonged. This is our appointed time to confess and come home. Let us confess together.

Confession

God, you call us, anoint us, and then send us out into the world. Often the cares of life tend to make us forget that we are not in charge of ourselves, but have been bought with the great price of the blood of the Lamb. Forgive us our sin. Wash us from the filth of ourselves. Make us yours, we pray, in the name of the one who purchased us.

Words of Assurance

The Good Shepherd has laid down his life for us. He knows his own. There is one flock. With our confession, we have one Shepherd. This is good news.

Responsive Reading

Leader: The psalmist did not write in the comfort of the royal palace.
People: The Lord is my Shepherd. I shall not want.
Leader: David wrote as he was on the lam, running for his life.
People: God makes us lie down in green pastures and leads us besides still waters.
Leader: The situations in David's life were turbulent and filled with anxious stress.
People: God restores our soul and leads us in the right paths for the sake of that great name.
Leader: David had been chosen to be king but couldn't get into the palace.
People: Even though we walk through deep valleys we don't have to fear evil, for God is with us.
Leader: David needed to encourage himself in the salvation of his God.
People: The rod of God and the staff of God offer us comfort.
Leader: Grief, anger, pain, and disappointment were served to David while he was running for his life.
People: God prepares a table for us in the very presence of our enemies and anoints us with healing oil. Our cup of joy overflows.
Leader: David was doing the business of being Church even while trying to remain alive.
People: Surely goodness and mercy shall follow us all the days of our lives and we shall dwell in the house of the Lord all our lives and even forevermore. This is our blessed assurance!

Offertory Invitation

Tabitha, called Dorcas, was devoted to good works and acts of loving kindness. When she became ill and died, the saints told the apostle that she had served God by serving them. The prayer of faith raised her up to live again. This story helps us to better understand that our giving is always unto God, who takes notice and grants us abundant life. Let's give.

Offertory Praise

Generous One, it is because of your great care for us that we have anything to offer you and your people. We give because you have promised that we will hunger nor thirst any more. You promised that the sun would not strike us nor any scorching heat, for the Lamb at the center of the throne will be our Shepherd and will guide us to springs of the water of life. We offer to take you at your Word, in the name of the Christ of Life.

Benediction

Leader: Little Sheep, return to the great numbers in the world.

People: We join the multitudes who come through every nation, all tribes and all people.

Leader: The family fold of Jesus Christ has one great hymn of praise.

People: We go, singing, "Salvation belongs to our God, who is seated on the throne, and to the Lamb."

Leader: Let your lights so shine before the world that they join in the glorious song.

People: Blessing and glory and wisdom and thanksgiving and honor and power and might be to our God forever and ever. Amen.

Leader: God the Banquet Giver, Christ the Lamb, and the Holy Spirit go before us!

People: Thanks be to God! Amen.

FIFTH SUNDAY OF EASTER

Acts 11:1–18
Psalm 148
Revelation 21:1–6
John 13:31–35

Call to Worship

Leader: The Gift of Love summons our gathering.
People: We offer Love thanks for the gift of families and community.
Leader: The Gift of Love calls us to extend the gift to the unlovable and unlovely.
People: We who were lost in sin, wandering far from home, were accepted because of Love.
Leader: The Gift of Love so inspires us to follow the commandment of Love.
People: Because we are loved, we come to offer love with joyful praise.

Call to Confession

We love because God first loved us. Those who say they love God and hate their brothers or sisters are liars. For we cannot love God, whom we have not seen, and hate those we see each day. Let us confess our sin.

Confession

Almighty God, Lover of our souls, we come to you with ruptured relationships everywhere. Breathe upon us the breath of new life. Forgive us our sin. Help us to love in deeds that reveal your presence in our lives. Empower us to walk in the new life of the Christ, in whose name we pray.

Words of Assurance

God has given us a new commandment that we love one another. Just as God has loved us, we ought also love one another. By this everyone will know that we are disciples, if we have love one for another. God loves us. God forgives us. This is good news.

Responsive Reading

Leader: Love is an action word!

People: May we love one another in both word and deed.

Leader: Love cannot be silent.

People: Love created the world as a birthday gift for human inhabitants.

Leader: Love spoke to the rest of the world, but stooped down and hand-crafted the living creatures with tenderness, affection, and gentleness.

People: We are each individually fashioned in the image of Love and gifted with intellect and a soul.

Leader: Love came to visit with the creatures of clay every day. Personal contact with dirt was essential to Love.

People: Love knew that rebellion and sin would interrupt this awesome intimacy between the human and the Divine. But Love had already provided a way of escape from everlasting death.

Leader: Love put on human flesh, stepped on a down escalator, and eased into our community.

People: Love role modeled for us the way those who have the image of God in them behave!

Leader: Love marched to Calvary with dignity and died our death.

People: Love was lifted from the stench of death and now has an appointed place at the right hand of God, interceding for us to keep rising and moving on in love. We can do it, for we have that same Love poured into our heart by the Holy Spirit. Love continues to lift. We call out a shout for the Love that never fails.

Offertory Invitation

Beloved, let us love one another, because love is from God. Everyone who loves is born of God and knows God. Whoever does not love does not know God, for God is love. God's love has been revealed to us through the life, death, and resurrection of God's only begotten Son. Our sacrificial giving is the only appropriate response.

Offertory Praise

God, it is by your Holy Spirit that we give. In generosity you have given unto us. Receive now our gifts to be used for others. In the name of Lavish Love, we pray.

Benediction

Leader: Jesus is the Sending Agent!

People: We leave, knowing that God is among mortals.

Leader: God dwells with us and we belong to God.

People: God will wipe every tear from our eyes.

Leader: The power of death has been broken.

People: Mourning and crying shall be wiped away, and pain will be no more.

Leader: God is the Alpha and the Omega, the Beginning and the End, knowing the end before the beginning. Go in confidence, act in faith, and dwell in Love.

People: Thanks be to God. Amen.

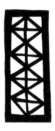

SIXTH SUNDAY OF EASTER

Acts 16:9–15
Psalm 67
Revelation 21:10–22:5
John 14:23–29 or John 5:1–9

Call to Worship

Leader: We gather to practice for living in the Holy City, where the temple is the Almighty and the Lamb.

People: The City has no need of sun or moon to shine on it, for the glory of God is its light, and its lamp is the Lamb.

Leader: The nations will walk by its light.

People: People will bring into it the glory and honor of every nation.

Leader: But nothing unclean will enter there. No one who practices abomination or falsehood will be admitted.

People: Only those whose names are written in the Lamb's Book of Life will be admitted.

Leader: The river of the Water of Life, bright as crystal, flows from the throne of God and of the Lamb.

People: On either side of the river is the Tree of Life and the leaves are for the healing of the nations.

Leader: Nothing accursed will be found there any more.

People: We don't want to be left behind! We gather now to practice true worship before the throne. We will worship in spirit and in truth.

Call to Confession

Those who love Jesus keep his words. Those who do not love Jesus will do whatever they feel is right. If we make it to the Holy City, it is because we have been faithful to the leading of the Holy Spirit, who never leads us astray. Let's use this time to get right with God.

Confession

God, we have sinned. We have compared ourselves with other humans and looked fairly good to ourselves. But when we hear and read and comprehend the words of the Revelator, we know that our past week's behaviors will not win for us admission to the Holy City. Forgive us. Cleanse us. Fill us with your powerful Holy Spirit, we pray in the name of the Lamb of Life.

Words of Assurance

The Advocate, the Holy Spirit, whom God sent in the name of Jesus Christ, teaches us everything and reminds us of what Jesus has said. The words are alive today: "Peace, I leave with you. My peace I give to you. I do not give to you as the world gives. Do not let your hearts be troubled, and do not let them be afraid. You have heard me say to you that I am going away and I am coming to you." This is the promise of our Promise Keeper. It is good news.

Responsive Reading

Leader: People of God, we have been marked by God's blessings!
People: True dat. True dat. For we have no other answers for the ways that have been made for us.
Leader: Hemmed in, backed into corners, and having our backs up against the walls, we have been continually brought out by God. God has made ways when there seemed to be no ways.
People: Thrown to the curb, kicked aside, left behind, and walked over, still we keep getting up.
Leader: We give out a shout for the Way Maker.
People: The Holy Spirit has pulled, pushed, and poked us along, whispering encouragement along the way.
Leader: When we wanted to sing the blues, the notes would not come out right.
People: High ways have come down. Low ways took a turn up. Storm clouds gave way to Sonshine. And the sour notes took on a life of their own.
Leader: Doors that were shut in our face swung open.
People: Miracle after miracle has taken place in spite of our messing up.
Leader: The cooling waters of our baptism held us until the Holy Spirit filled our hearts with wisdom.

People: The Spirit of the Living God has free course in our lives. We celebrate the indwelling presence of the Getting-on-up God.

Offertory Invitation

The news of our faith began outside of Jerusalem with a woman named Lydia and her group of women, who met on the Sabbath day at the waters to pray. Paul gave her the good news of Jesus and she invited them to come and share her home. Our giving today will allow us to spread the same news of Jesus and invite others to come along and follow us "home." Let's give liberally.

Offertory Praise

God, Sister Lydia dealt in purple cloth, and our exchange is money. We, like she, offer you what we have to share so that others might journey with us to the Holy City. We give these gifts, with thanksgiving, in the Name Above Every Name.

Benediction

Leader: May God be gracious to us and bless us.
People: May the face of God shine upon us.
Leader: Let the way of God be made known upon the earth.
People: We leave to share God's saving power among all the nations.
Leader: Be glad and sing for joy. Our God judges people with equity and guides the nations.
People: We leave with songs of confidence upon our lips, for our God reigns.
Leader: May God continue to bless us and all the earth give reverence. Go in peace.
People: Amen!

ASCENSION SUNDAY · SEVENTH SUNDAY AFTER EASTER

Acts 1:1–11
Psalm 47 or 110
Ephesians 1:15–23
Luke 24:44–53

Call to Worship

Leader: Clap your hands, all you people, and shout with loud songs of joy.
People: Our God is most awesome, a great God over all the earth.
Leader: Jesus ascended with a shout. Soon Jesus will return with trumpet sound.
People: We come to sing praises to our God.
Leader: Lift the deeds of God in worthy hymns. Let the anthems ring with celebration.
People: We have come to join the psalmist and offer worship to the One on the throne.
Leader: Jesus lifted his hands and blessed the crowd as he returned home, mission accomplished.
People: He sent back the Holy Spirit. We gather to be refreshed by the Latter Rain of Life.

Call to Confession

God has put all things under the feet of Jesus and has made him the head over all things for the Church, which is his body, the fullness of the one who fills all in all. We have moved away in the past week from the Ultimate Authority. Confession will repair our relationship. Shall we pray?

Confession

God, you have opened our minds to understand the Holy Scriptures. We read the law of Moses and quote it well. We marvel at the deeds you worked through the prophets and we are comforted by the Psalms. Yet we have sinned and come short of what we know. Forgive us our sin. Fill us with your Holy Spirit so we will not find ourselves in this place again, we pray in the name of the One who promised us this power.

Words of Assurance

Thus it is written that the Messiah was to suffer and to rise from the dead on the third day, and that repentance and forgiveness of sins is to be proclaimed in his name to all nations. We are witnesses of these things. This is our time of a fresh start.

Responsive Reading

Leader: It's time to stop playing Church. It's time to be the people of God.
People: God sits and waits on us to do the greater works of Jesus Christ!
Leader: Jesus is our chief cheerleader, applauding our steps of faith.
People: The angels yearn to throw a party in celebration of our making God look good in the earth.
Leader: The Holy Spirit was given to help us do the exploits that make the world take notice.
People: We have made the Holy Spirit a denomination and put limits on the power of God.
Leader: We have a live-in companion, a comforter, teacher, and power blast wrestling to be turned loose on our behalf!
People: God has already subdued the nations and preserved them as our heritage, while we sit and whine about what we don't have.
Leader: We can overcome with a simple request.
People: Holy Spirit, reign in me. I surrender my will and offer you control. Work in me. Work on me. Work through me. Take the first place in my walk with Jesus Christ and make me a winner for God's realm. I welcome you this day as the power in my life. Clothe me with that holy power from on high. I yield to your guidance this day and every day. I receive you in the matchless name of Christ, the Wonder Worker.

Offertory Invitation

We know the hope to which we have been called as the riches of God and a glorious inheritance among the saints. The immeasurable greatness of God's power has been given to those of us who believe, according to the working of the Holy Spirit in our lives. For this reason alone, we can give with joy.

Offertory Praise

God, we have heard of your love toward all the saints. And we have experienced your love in our lives. So, with gratitude for your faithfulness, we give so that others might come to know you. Receive our gifts in the name of the One seated at your right hand far above all rule, authority, power, and dominion and above every name that is named, not only in this age, but also in the age to come, we pray.

Benediction

Leader: Leave, knowing that it is now up to us!
People: The realm of God has been left in our hands.
Leader: God has already shown us love by sending Jesus to die for our sin.
People: Jesus has shown his love by dying and rising on our behalf.
Leader: Jesus ascended upon high and sent back the Holy Spirit to work in our lives.
People: We have been called and filled with power from on high.
Leader: John baptized with water, but the Holy Spirit now reigns, giving us a spirit of revelation and wisdom.
People: We leave to be change agents in the world that we touch.
Leader: The God of opportunities, the Christ of possibilities, and the Promised Holy Spirit are ours!
People: Hallelujah and amen!

SEVENTH SUNDAY OF EASTER

Acts 16:16–34
Psalm 97
Revelation 22:12–14, 16–17, 20–21
John 17:20–26

Call to Worship

Leader: Slaves of the Most High God!
People: We are present for our new assignments.
Leader: Slaves of the Ancient of Days!
People: We are present for rejoicing in our God!
Leader: Slaves of the Omnipotent God!
People: We are present to give praise to Jesus Christ.
Leader: Slaves of the Alpha and the Omega!
People: We are present to be filled with the Holy Spirit.
Leader: Slaves of the Pillar and Ground of Truth!
People: We are present to offer our whole selves in worship unto our God!

Call to Confession

John the Revelator heard Christ proclaim: "See, I am coming soon; my reward is with me, to repay according to everyone's work. I am the Alpha and the Omega, the first and the last, the beginning and the end. Blessed are those who wash their robes, so that they will have the right to the tree of life and may enter the city by the gates." Confession washes us clean. Let us pray.

Confession

God, we know that your return is imminent. Yet, the folly of the world continues to hold our attention. The loud voices that call seem so appealing and tend to get our attention more quickly than your still, soft voice. Forgive us our sin. We want to be ready to meet you when the trumpet sounds and you break through the clouds. We pray in the name of Steadfast Hope.

Words of Assurance

The Holy Spirit and the Bride bid us to come. Everyone who is thirsty, come. Let anyone who wishes take the Water of Life as a gift. This is good news.

Responsive Reading

Leader: Prayer and praise summon the Divine Healer!

People: Clouds of depression, thick storms of despair, and the onslaughts of desolation must give way when we pray.

Leader: The foundations of prayer are right living and doing justice in the world.

People: Prayer strikes the heavens like an earthquake! The angels are dispatched when we pray.

Leader: Mountains melt. Prisoners are released. Doors open. Chains are unfastened as we pray.

People: Look at how the elements ring out the majesty of God. God's glory is so inclusive!

Leader: All the noisy things that vex our spirits are quieted in our times of prayer.

People: Great is the comfort of all who dare to have a little talk with Jesus.

Leader: We overcome our trials when we share the praise reports of our answered prayers.

People: Bowing before other altars is both foolish and in vain. Only God is worthy of our prayers.

Leader: Our hearts are made glad when God dispatches help in all of our situations and with all of our issues.

People: Those who hate evil and refuse to participate in wrong are loved by God, who answers prayer.

Leader: Prayer places a hedge of protection around us and all of our circumstances.

People: Prayers reach way beyond our scope of imagination, for we serve an exceedingly, abundantly above-and-beyond God, who delights in giving us the desires of our hearts.

Leader: Many times our prayers have kept us from snares, plots, and unknown wicked schemes.

People: Prayer brings about a shift in our perspective and, often, delight to our hearts. We rejoice in the God who initiated a prayerful relationship with us.

Offertory Invitation

Jesus prayed for us before giving his life. He prayed not only for the apostles who were in his immediate circle, but on behalf of all who would believe in him through the witness of others. He prayed that we who are known would be in community even with those we don't know. For we are family. We share, knowing that the world is connected in the Body of Christ.

Offertory Praise

God, by the witness of their lives, an unbeliever came to ask the apostles, "What must I do to be saved?" They answered, "Believe on the Lord Jesus, and you will be saved, you and your household." As the household of yours is worldwide, we offer our gifts to you that families everywhere might come to know Christ, in whose name we pray.

Benediction

Leader: Jesus Christ is surely coming soon. Be ready when he comes.
People: Amen. Come, Lord Jesus.
Leader: The grace of the Lord Jesus be with all the saints. The truth of God, the love of Christ, and the power of the Holy Spirit go with us.
People: Hallelujah and amen.

6 · PENTECOST AND THE FOLLOWING SEASON

The Holy Spirit arrives fresh, hot, touching, laughing, anointing, and dispatching the hidden and scared individuals into the streets. The Holy Spirit, the Comforter, sent to live in us, work on us, walk beside us to guide our daily life, comes on the scene. It's time for celebration. It's a distinct and significant occasion, for power is in the house! It's a brand new day, a brand new beginning, and a brand new season of growth, spread, and change.

"You'll receive power" is the promise of Acts 1:8. The Holy Spirit's power is necessary for the effective living of our new life in Christ. The acts and deeds of those called Christian will be noticed by all the world. The power to make a difference is ours!

Ordinary time—the long period between Pentecost and Advent—is the longest season of the Church, where we are called to live out our faith on a daily basis without any festival to celebrate. As we walk with God on a daily basis, in the mundane duties of regular existence, the worship rituals, our daily devotions, and our life of prayer will see us through.

Altar Focus

For Pentecost, red with white paraments and red balloons are needed to set the stage for fire, which not only burns and consumes, but ignites, motivates, and inspires. Red candles of assorted sizes and shapes would make a lovely addition. A banner with tongues of fire laid across the altar can assist in delivering the message of a brand new day.

The liturgical color for ordinary time is green to signify growth, which God continues to anticipate from our lives as we live without fanfare and hoopla.

PENTECOST SUNDAY

Acts 2:1–21 or Genesis 11:1–9
Psalm 104:24–35b
Romans 8:14–17
John 14:8–17, 25–27

Call to Worship

Leader: When the Day of Pentecost had come, they were all together in one place.

People: And suddenly from heaven there came a sound like the rush of a violent wind.

Leader: It filled the entire house where they were sitting. Divided tongues of fire appeared among them and a tongue rested on each of them.

People: All of them were filled with the Holy Spirit and began to speak in tongues as the Spirit gave them ability.

Leader: People of God, I declare that when we get it together, the Holy Spirit shows up!

People: Spirit of the Living God, fall afresh on us. We gather, ready to worship and to receive!

Call to Confession

All who are led by the Holy Spirit of God are the children of God. For God's children do not receive a spirit of slavery to fall back into fear, but we have received a spirit of adoption, which makes us like Jesus Christ. For the many sins we have committed, forgetting our adoption, let us pray.

Confession

God, you have called us your children, and we have misrepresented your love and your grace. Jesus told us that we would do even greater works than he did while upon the earth; yet in our fear, we continue to major in minor issues and little things. We have sinned. Forgive us, we pray, in the name of the One Who Loves Us Best!

Words of Assurance

When we cry, "Abba, Parent God," it is the very Holy Spirit, bearing witness with our spirit that we are children of God, and if children, then heirs, heirs of God and joint heirs with Christ. This is certainly good news.

Responsive Reading

Leader: People, we need to get it together!

People: When the whole earth had one language and the same words, God came to see about the people.

Leader: And what did God say about those who had it going on together?

People: God said, "Look, they are one people, and they have all one language; and this is only the beginning of what they will do; nothing that they propose to do will now be impossible for them!"

Leader: Suddenly, there was the sound of babbling, for the people began to speak in different tongues!

People: The people were bewildered, amazed, and astonished as they began to go their separate ways.

Leader: What happened on the Day of Pentecost?

People: God gave the Church a common language! All the world was able again to hear the same words.

Leader: With the coming of the Holy Spirit we can get it together!

People: With the coming of the Holy Spirit we are sent forth into all the world to build lives in love.

Leader: The God of great works is honored when we get it together as believers.

People: There is none like God, whose wisdom created from nothing all that is our world.

Leader: Water, water, everywhere and the supply is inexhaustible.

People: Tiny ants, small weeds and shrubs, gnats and jumping fleas each have God's concern.

Leader: Whales, dolphins, elephants, and giant redwoods were all designed with care by God.

People: Seed time, harvest, forest fires, and raging floods don't destroy the works of God's hand.

Leader: Their creation was complete before they came forth.

People: If God ever went sour on us again, as at Babel, the world would crumble.

Leader: The gentle and strong winds are simple reminders of the Breath of God, the Holy Spirit.

People: God is a renewing, refreshing, and regenerating Spirit.

Leader: May the glory of our God endure forever. May God always rejoice in the creation.

People: Our prayers of praise are magnified as we consider God's limitless reach and span.

Leader: Our limited musical abilities pale when we attempt to bless God's movements in song.

People: Yet, from the rising of the sun to the going down of the same, the Holy Spirit prompts the praise of God to reign in our being. For God is all that!

Offertory Invitation

"In the last days it will be," God declares, "that I will pour out my spirit upon all flesh, and your sons and your daughters shall prophesy, and your young men shall see visions and your old men shall dream dreams. Even upon my slaves, both men and women, in those days I will pour out my Spirit and they shall prophesy." The foretelling of God's glory demands that we share so that the whole world may come to know Christ.

Offertory Praise

The Advocate has come and, God, we give you praise, for we heard the news in our own language. So that others might have this privilege, please accept our gifts in the name of the One about whom the Holy Spirit testifies.

Benediction

Leader: Jesus told the disciples: "I have said these things to you while I am still with you. But the Advocate, the Holy Spirit whom God will send in my name, will teach you everything, and remind you of all that I have said to you. Peace I leave with you; my peace I give to you. I do not give to you as the world gives. Do not let your hearts be troubled, and do not let them be afraid." Go forth in the name of the peace of God, the presence of Christ, and the power of the Holy Spirit.

People: Hallelujah and amen.

TRINITY SUNDAY · FIRST SUNDAY AFTER PENTECOST

Proverbs 8:1–4, 22–31
Psalm 8
Romans 5:1–5
John 16:12–15

Call to Worship

Leader: The voice of Wisdom has called us!
People: We have understood the sister's call and come to discover more wise ways to live.
Leader: Wisdom is a woman created by God before earth's formation.
People: She danced, clapped, and applauded as God played in the dirt.
Leader: The ancients revered her counsel and embraced her as a sage.
People: She is not shy or retiring, but loud, bold, and sassy as she calls us to God!
Leader: God is here! The Triune God is present!
People: We have gathered with Wisdom to worship and adore the God of Yesterday, Today, and Forevermore!

Call to Confession

Before the mountains were shaped or the hills laid in place, before the earth and fields were created or the night separated from the day, the Trinity shared their divine image, wisdom, and intellect with us. Yet we have failed to behave in ways that give them glory. Let us confess.

Confession

Triune God, you continue to come to us and to call forth the very best from us. We fall down. We forget our destiny. We fail to heed your call. Forgive our sin. Restore us in the name of the Only Begotten Son.

Words of Assurance

Therefore, since we are justified by faith, we have peace with God through our Lord Jesus Christ, through whom we have obtained access to this grace in which we stand. This is mighty good news.

Responsive Reading

Leader: Sovereign. Our God is Sovereign!

People: There is none like God, the three in one, who decided to visit earth in three different forms.

Leader: The Holy Sovereign played in the dirt and then had daily communion with the dirt creatures.

People: They were naked and didn't know it. Their innocence allowed them to face God without shame or guilt. Then the sin of rebellion won their attention.

Leader: So God decided to put on their skin, walk in their shoes, and live in their community as Jesus.

People: But the sin of rebellion continued to reign, for we hung God on a tree as a sinful being!

Leader: The Risen Christ showed up and showed out, sovereign.

People: As he ascended back to the heavens, he promised to send the Holy Spirit to live in us and to guide us all the way home. What an Awesome God!

Offertory Invitation

The whole wide world belongs to God. The creation is a masterpiece and we are allowed to have dominion over the works of God's own hands. Our responsibility includes sharing so that others have what they need to live.

Offertory Praise

God, the skies, the seas, the mountains, the valleys, and the creatures have a way of saying "thanks." Thank you for sending the powerful winds of the Holy Spirit upon our lives so that giving has become our loving response. Receive these gifts in the name of your Conquering Son, we pray.

Benediction

Leader: The Triune God sits enthroned forever. Now, may the Eternal Trinity grant us strength and bless us all with great shalom!

People: Hallelujah and amen.

PROPER 4 · SUNDAY BETWEEN MAY 29 AND JUNE 4

1 Kings 18:20–39 or 1 Kings 8:22–23, 41–43
Psalm 96 or Psalm 96:1–9
Galatians 1:1–12
Luke 7:1–10

Call to Worship

Leader: The Voice, the Answer, and the Response await us.
People: We are not worthy to come into this place of sacred sanctuary.
Leader: The Voice has called you clearly to come.
People: Our complex lives are in need of the Answer.
Leader: The Response to the many needs of our lives is present to minister.
People: We await the fire of the Holy Spirit to fall fresh upon us in our time of worship.
Leader: We do not presume upon the Holy One. Yet, we have been called.
People: Only speak the Word and let us, God's servants, be healed.

Call to Confession

We, like the prophets of Baal, choose the wrong gods. We have served many gods this week and found ourselves empty and alone. It's time to pull down the altars that do not bring us salvation and ask forgiveness of our sin. Shall we pray?

Confession

How many times have we stumbled and fallen this week, Great God? How many times have we neglected to call upon your grace, but rather we have slipped and slid, trying to do it with our little hidden gods. Yet, we have heard your call. We know you are the answer. We know your response when we confess our sin. And we have sinned. Cleanse us with your grace, we pray, in the name of Jesus Christ.

Words of Assurance

It was God who rained down fire upon the altar of Baal. When all the people saw it, they fell on their faces and said, "The Lord indeed is God." The fire has fallen upon us because the Lord indeed is our God. This is our pardon and our consolation.

Responsive Reading

Leader: Let's sing unto God a fresh melody. Let's tell of God's goodness with lyrics of praise.

People: That would be all good. But first we must come together and decide what type of new song we want to sing.

Leader: Open wide your mouths and allow the melody to rise within you.

People: Yes, there is a melody that connects us all. It comes from our experiences of amazing grace.

Leader: So, what's wrong with lining out a metered hymn?

People: We need to take apart the chords. We need to check the scales. We need to look at the movements that gave us a song in the first place.

Leader: Taking apart the chords sounds like destruction. We have come to worship.

People: Chords are simply notes put together in order to produce a quality sound. Chords are the blending of different strains to illustrate the movement you feel within. We need to take apart the standard chords.

Leader: Well, let's hear the different chords to the new song!

People: We have a collective consciousness about the times that have passed. It's yesterday, today, and tomorrow that we need to consider before we sing.

Leader: What is so different from the days of our ancestors? They sang wonderful spirituals, hymns, and anthems.

People: They sang of their lived experiences with God. Many of their words describe us too. Yet, we have some new experiences that demand new notes of praise.

Leader: Give the world an accounting of the honor and majesty due God's name.

People: We have been kept through dangers, seen and unseen. Our children have not been given over to the drug lords or violent gangs.

Leader: Our seniors are respected and have decent places to live. Our jobs have not been downsized or sent overseas.

People: We have positions our parents never imagined and a technical world that none of them could even conceive. And through it all God keeps on doing great things for us, with us, to us, through us, and in spite of us.

Leader: Only God could keep our families secure and give us enough love to bind us together.

People: The chords, the melodies, nor the lyrics can express our thankfulness. We can only hum and sigh in gratitude. God hears and understands.

Offertory Invitation

The psalmist declares that we are to give God the glory and to bring an offering worthy of God when we come into the sanctuary. Let us worship God in holy splendor as we share of our resources in the offering.

Offertory Praise

God, we worship you as Sovereign. The heavens adore you, the earth rejoices before you, even the sea and the fields pay you homage. You are coming to judge the world with righteousness and your people with truth. Please receive these, our offerings, as a sign of our adoration and praise. We pray in the name of the One Soon to Come.

Benediction

Leader: Grace to you and peace from God and the Lord Jesus Christ, who gave himself for our sins to set us free from the present evil age.

People: We leave to speak this word in all the places we will go this week.

Leader: Go, according to the divine will and purpose of the Voice, the Answer, and the Response.

People: Hallelujah and amen.

PROPER 5 · SUNDAY BETWEEN JUNE 5 AND JUNE 11

1 Kings 17:8–16, (17–24) or 1 Kings 17:7–24
Psalm 146 or Psalm 30
Galatians 1:11–24
Luke 7:11–17

Call to Worship

Leader: Compassion is in this house!
People: We're thankful, for we have experienced meanness this past week.
Leader: Mercy is present to have free course.
People: We're grateful, for mercy suits our case.
Leader: The spirit of healing is ready to comfort.
People: We give thanks that the Balm of Gilead continues to flow for us.
Leader: The time of praise and thanksgiving has arrived.
People: We have gathered to worship the God who cares!

Call to Confession

God supplied every need of a widowed African woman in Zarephath who was parenting and trying to provide for her son in a famine. God had mercy upon a widow whose only source of income, her son, had died and was on the way to be buried. Both the Hebrew text and the New Testament testify to the compassion, mercy, healing, and provision of God. Yet we continue to stray, seeking other lovers. Let's take this time to confess.

Confession

God, we are as dead as the young man in the coffin without the life you provide. We are just as doomed as Elijah by the dry river and the widow with a little oil and flour without your grace. We have sinned. We ask forgiveness. Hear our prayer, in the name of Compassion.

Words of Assurance

The Lord listens to our confessions and knows our hearts. With genuine repentance new life is breathed into us and we are revived. This is good news.

Responsive Reading

Leader: Worship is always a wake-up call.

People: We want to hear the words that will bring new life to our spirits.

Leader: Well, don't depend on humans and their frail existence.

People: All around us our idols and stars are dying. The work they have done seems to dry up like dust.

Leader: Our only help is in the capable and dependable hands of God.

People: Our hope is built upon the God of the ancestors. This is a strong God who never fails.

Leader: God made the world and all that's in it. God has provided for the creation.

People: God continues to make time for the little and weak ones of the world.

Leader: Food time and harvest time happen over and over again.

People: Most of our best times happen over meals eaten together. It's communion and community.

Leader: God continues to go our bail.

People: God keeps giving us sight to see what has been invisible before.

Leader: We walk with our heads up and our hands lifted in praise.

People: God's provision is legendary; we are some mighty blessed folks.

Leader: In our community there are no strangers. We welcome and accept all whom God made and loves.

People: We are grateful for the love of God that enfolds us on every leaning side and props a fence of protection all around us. There is none like the Compassionate Savior. We pledge allegiance to this God forevermore.

Offertory Invitation

Brothers and sisters, the gospel has not been proclaimed or preserved for us through human origin; for we did not receive it from a human source but through a revelation of Jesus Christ. So that this divine revelation might be shared around the world, we give generously.

Offertory Praise

God, we have given as you commanded, dependent upon your promise that the jars of meal will not be emptied and the jugs of oil will not fail in our homes. We give in the name of the Spirit of Anticipation.

Benediction

Leader: Go into the world with compassion.

People: We leave to be compassionate to all we meet.

Leader: Go into the world with mercy.

People: We will be merciful to even the unmerciful. We ask God's help.

Leader: Go into the world, heal the sick, and raise the dead.

People: We leave to do the greater works in the name of the Voice, the Answer, and the Response. Hallelujah and amen.

PROPER 6 · SUNDAY BETWEEN JUNE 12 AND JUNE 18

1 Kings 21:1–10, (11–14), 15–21a or 2 Samuel 11:26–12:10, 13–15
Psalm 5:1–8 or Psalm 32
Galatians 2:15–21
Luke 7:36–8:3

Call to Worship

Leader: The spirit of death has driven us here.
People: We have been in a fight with evil all week long.
Leader: There are yet many who want to deny us freedom.
People: The God of Liberty breaks through the plots and plans of death.
Leader: God speaks into our lives with incessant calls for the right to create and to be free.
People: We praise the God of New Days, New Life, and New Seasons!

Call to Confession

When we sell ourselves to do what is evil in the sight of God, we bring disaster upon ourselves. This is our time to confess our sin and get right with God. Shall we pray?

Confession

God, we know that a person is justified not by the works of the law, but through faith in Jesus Christ. And we have come to believe in Christ Jesus so that we might be justified by our faith. However, we continue to return to the things we have left and continue to do the things we hate. Forgive our sin. Fix us to stand before you without guilt or stain, we pray in the name of the Anointed One.

Words of Assurance

Our sins that were many have been forgiven. See what love God has for us—while we were sinners, Christ died for us. Our faith in him has saved us. This is good news!

Responsive Reading

Leader: Do what you have the power to do for God.
People: Sometimes we feel like Naboth, set up to fall!
Leader: Do what you have the power to do for God.
People: Sometimes we feel like Elijah, given harsh words to speak to power brokers.
Leader: Do what you have the power to do for God.
People: Sometimes we feel like the woman who anointed Christ, talked about for giving what we have to offer.
Leader: Do what you have the power to do for God.
People: The wicked will reap their just reward from God.
Leader: Do what you have the power to do for God.
People: God takes care of the liars, the bloodthirsty, the deceitful.
Leader: Do what you have the power to do for God.
People: We will live for God, tell of God's goodness, and enter the house of God with awe. For we are led in paths of righteousness despite the deeds of our enemies. We are daily given godly strength and will do what we have the power to do for God.

Offertory Invitation

We walk by faith and not by sight! Our giving results in outcomes we cannot see. Yet it is because of our faith that we will generously share our gifts.

Offertory Praise

God, each of us must appear before the judgment seat of Christ. Receive now the works of our hands that it might be willing thanks for all you have given us. In the name of Matchless Love we pray.

Benediction

Leader: Go into the world, knowing the reverence of God.
People: We leave to persuade others by our lives.
Leader: Go into the world, boasting of the mighty deeds God.
People: We leave to give God praise by our activities this week.
Leader: Go into the world, knowing that the old has passed away.
People: We leave remembering we are new creations in Christ.
Leader: The blessings of the Ancient of Days, the Redeemer of Souls, and the Holy Spirit will make every day a new beginning.
People: Hallelujah and amen!

PROPER 7 · JUNETEENTH OBSERVATION
SUNDAY BETWEEN JUNE 19 AND JUNE 25

1 Kings 19:1–4, (5–7), 8–15a or Isaiah 65:1–9
Psalm 42–43 or Psalm 22:19–28
Galatians 3:23–29
Luke 8:26–39

Call to Worship

Leader: The table is prepared!
People: We have come to eat and to be satisfied.
Leader: The food here satisfies and prepares us for the week to come.
People: We have met many Jezebels and Ahabs this past week, and the scent of death has been strong all around us.
Leader: The Maker of Bread, the Well of Living Water, and the Wine of Life are here.
People: We come to dine with sufficiency as we offer the sacrifice of worship and praise.

Call to Confession

The political threats are always present. The voices of those who seek our lives often tend to have us running away from conflict like the prophet Elijah. In our running we miss God. This is the time when we allow God to confront us as we confess.

Confession

God, we have been terrified of the Ahabs and Jezebels in our lives. Instead of running to you, we have allowed them to send us in the opposite directions. We have sinned. We have made others bigger in our eyes than you, the Sovereign God. Forgive us, we pray, in the name of Jesus Christ.

Words of Assurance

There is no longer Jew or Greek, there is no longer slave or free, there is no longer male or female; for all of us are one in Christ Jesus. And, since we belong to Christ, then we are Abraham's and Sarah's offspring, heirs according to the promise of God. It doesn't get any better than this! Thanks be to God.

Responsive Reading

Leader: There is no prettier sight than watching a tiny deer drink with grace at the watering hole.

People: We have been like that graceful deer, hungering to have deep, satisfying drinks of the Living Water. Our thirst cannot be satisfied any other way.

Leader: It seems that we have been on a diet of tears. Our stories are getting sadder, more wearying, and more difficult to comprehend.

People: We keep looking for the slightest signs of God. We keep asking each other, "Where is God?"

Leader: There is our common memory of gathering as the people of God with victory on our lips, praise in our hands, and shouting in our feet.

People: Those were the good old days! Today seems to be very different. Our collective soul is in misery for the pains that we bear. When it seems that we should almost have it made, we find ourselves in deeper and deeper holes. They are not watering holes. They seem more like pits!

Leader: Why is our soul cast down? Why are we upset? Where is our collective hope in God?

People: We have to call upon the days, the hours, and the times when God was there for us. We have to remember those days in order to bring rest to our anxious spirits.

Leader: Laments call to laments. Pain seeks our pain. Misery loves company!

People: We are not defeated! God has not left us alone. We are looking for the noise and excitement but God is working through the steady heartbeats, the rhythms of our pulse, and the quiet flow of blood through our veins. These are the sure signs of God's loving presence.

Leader: And yet we ask God, "Why have you forgotten about us? Why are we being constantly oppressed?"

People: It's called a test of our faith! Our souls get uneasy when we are forced to depend upon our faith. We want calm days and peaceful nights. Yet they don't bring God the glory that our going through these unsteady times brings. We live in hope to see the goodness of God! And it's all good! For God never fails!

Offertory Invitation

We work together with Christ to spread the good news. The Christ who is the Bread of Life, the Living Water, and the Table That Is Spread anticipates that we will do our part. Let's be generous in our giving.

Offertory Praise

God, we know too many folks who have no homes nor clothes. We know too many young men and women who are demon possessed. We know too many who are entombed in cemeteries they have built with their lives. We give to be a blessing to the bound, tormented, unclean spirits. Receive now our offerings in the name of the One who longs to set every captive free. Amen.

Benediction

Leader: The meal was prepared and you have eaten from the Table of Life. Return to your homes, your schools, your places of work and leisure, proclaiming throughout this city how much Jesus Christ has done for you.
People: Hallelujah and amen!

PROPER 8 · SUNDAY BETWEEN JUNE 26 AND JULY 2

2 Kings 2:1–2, 6–14 or 1 Kings 19:15–16, 19–21
Psalm 77:1–2 or Psalm 16, 11–20
Galatians 5:1, 13–25
Luke 9:51–62

Call to Worship

Leader: Where is the God of Elijah and the prophets?
People: We have come to seek a double portion of their anointing.
Leader: This is the place and the hour to worship.
People: We have heard of the joyful reports that God does wonders in the earth.
Leader: That same God is our God and wants to give away the mantle of power.
People: We come to see, to touch, to hear, and to be touched with power divine as we worship in spirit and in truth.

Call to Confession

We have been called to freedom, brothers and sisters, and have used our freedom as an opportunity for self-indulgence. The whole law is summed up in a single commandment, "You shall love the Lord your God with all your heart, mind, and strength, and your neighbor as yourself." For the many ways we have sinned, let us confess.

Confession

Generous God, your Word declares that the works of the flesh are obvious and not according to your will for our lives. We have been warned time and time again. Yet, we do the very things we hate. Forgive our sin. We pray in the name of the Crucified One.

Words of Assurance

The fruit of the Spirit is love, joy, peace, patience, kindness, generosity, faithfulness, gentleness, and self-control. There is no law against such things.

And we who belong to Christ Jesus have now crucified the flesh with its passions and desires. This is good news.

Responsive Reading

Leader: God knows that we cannot be quiet and appropriate with our calls for help. Many days our lives seem to be falling apart right in front of our faces.

People: We seek for God in trouble and it seems to get worse. We can't even be comfortable in the night; our dreams are troubled.

Leader: We are talking to ourselves. We know that we need help! We have nowhere else to go!

People: There is no god like our God. We know the stories; we have our own personal testimonies.

Leader: We know that God is a wonder worker.

People: We know the power of God's strong arm.

Leader: We know that God is a way maker.

People: We know that God hears and answers our prayers.

Leader: The changing seasons speak of a faithful God.

People: We see the majesty of God all around us. We yearn to see the exhibit of God's might on our behalf again.

Leader: God did great things for the biblical characters. God did great things for the ancestors. We are looking for an encore!

People: Our Red Seas need to be parted. The Pharaohs in our life need to be destroyed. We're standing at the banks of our own troubled waters saying, "Do it again, God! Do it again!"

Offertory Invitation

No one who puts the hand to the plow of salvation and looks back is fit for the realm of God. We have started a journey with Christ. Our giving in offerings is only one indication that we are looking forward and not turning back. Let's give generously so that the plan of salvation might continue to spread throughout the world.

Offertory Praise

For freedom, Christ has set us free. We are standing firm in our giving and not submitting again to the yokes of slavery. God, we share out of grateful hearts. Receive our offerings, given in the name of the One who set us free.

Benediction

Leader: Go! Set your face to do the work of God in the world.

People: Many will not receive us, yet we go to spread good news.

Leader: Go! Be prepared for the many excuses they will offer to deny Christ.

People: We will call them, by our lives, to follow the way to the Living Word.

Leader: Go in the creative energy of God, the ready compassion of Christ, and the enriching touch of the Holy Spirit. The power to make a difference is yours.

People: Hallelujah and amen!

PROPER 9 · SUNDAY BETWEEN JULY 3 AND JULY 9

2 Kings 5:1–14 or Isaiah 66:10–14
Psalm 30 or Psalm 66:1–9
Galatians 6:(1–6), 7–16
Luke 10:1–11, 16–20

Call to Worship

Leader: Come and hear the news of a little slave girl who saved a military chief's life.
People: We come to be reminded of what we can do with our lives.
Leader: Come and hear how we can share one another's burdens.
People: We come to be reminded of what is expected of our lives.
Leader: Come and hear the warnings about reaping and sowing.
People: We come to offer worship and praise so that the blessing of God might be sown into our lives. It's time for our lives to be stirred again.

Call to Confession

My friends, if anyone is detected in a transgression, we who have received the Spirit should restore such a one in the spirit of gentleness. Take care that we ourselves are not tempted. We are to bear one another's burdens so that we fulfill the law of Christ. For those of us who are nothing think that we are something and we deceive ourselves. It's confession time in this house.

Confession

God of the little slave girl who represented you so well, we have fallen far short of her example. We have wished our enemies a cruel death. We have kept our mouths shut about the Healing Balm that we know. Forgive us our sin. Make us like that little girl and use us in your service. We pray in the name of the Healer.

Words of Assurance

Let us not grow weary in doing what is right, for we will reap at harvest time if we do not give up. So, then, whenever we have an opportunity, let us work for the good of all, and especially for those of the family of faith. This is a mighty Word!

Responsive Reading

Leader: On the freeways and highways of life there are many wrecks and casualties.

People: God's grace has preserved our lives.

Leader: In hard times and bad situations we have had to yell quickly to God, "Help!"

People: God has always come to our rescue, especially when the circumstances were over our heads.

Leader: When the enemy felt that we were down for the count . . .

People: God stepped in, pulled us up, turned us around, and removed our feet from the slime of the pits.

Leader: Today we will offer God serious thanksgiving for sparing our sometimes worthless lives.

People: As our parent, God could have gotten tired of our foolishness and been done with our rebellious spirits.

Leader: But God's anger is only for a moment. Like that of a loving parent, God's favor is ours forever.

People: Our weeping may linger for the night, but joy comes with the morning.

Leader: And what do we want to say to the on-time God?

People: We shall not be moved, like trees planted by the ever-flowing stream; we shall not be moved from our faith in God!

Leader: We are as secure in God's goodness as a mountain firmly held in its place.

People: Mountains cannot offer God the verbal praise that we will give to the world. They are tall and impressive, but they are silent in their praise. We will rejoice, we will offer praise, we will call out a shout—for God is our present help and we will not keep quiet! We celebrate our worthy God! Glory! Glory! Glory!

Offertory Invitation

God has turned our mourning into dancing, taken burdens off our backs, and given us joy in place of our despair. Our giving is a silent but significant way of shouting back our thanks.

Offertory Praise

God, we have not grown weary in our doing what is right, for you have promised and we believe and have even experienced reaping great harvest from our investments in your realm. So we give as giving unto you. We pray that your peace, your grace, and your joy be multiplied upon all who are the recipients of these gifts that we offer in the name of Jesus Christ.

Benediction

Leader: Go into the world knowing that the harvest is plentiful but the laborers are few.
People: We are sent on our way as lambs into the midst of wolves.
Leader: Go into the world and bid all you encounter God's shalom.
People: We leave to proclaim Christ as the All That of our lives.
Leader: God the Grower, Christ the Vine, and the Holy Spirit, the Harvest Giver, go before us!
People: Hallelujah and amen.

PROPER 10 · SUNDAY BETWEEN JULY 10 AND JULY 16

Amos 7:7–17 or Deuteronomy 30:9–14
Psalm 82 or Psalm 25:1–10
Colossians 1:1–14
Luke 10:25–37

Call to Worship

Leader: Grace to you and peace from God, our authority and standard setter.

People: We gather with hearts of thanksgiving for our common faith in Jesus, our model of excellence.

Leader: Because of the hope we have in the Everlasting Arm, we have peace with God.

People: This is our time to lean again upon the resources of the Trinity, the Living Word, and the songs of Zion. We come to worship and offer heartfelt praise.

Call to Confession

The saints of the ages have prayed for us that we might be filled with the knowledge of God's will in all spiritual wisdom and understanding, so that we would live lives worthy of God and fully pleasing to the One who called us and saved us by grace. Since we have not lived up to what we know, this is our time of confession.

Confession

God, you have called us to bear fruit in every good work and to grow in our knowledge of you. You continually give us opportunities to be made strong with all the strength that comes from your glorious power. We have failed many tests this past week. We have sinned. We ask your forgiveness in the name of your beloved son, Jesus.

Words of Assurance

With our confessions we have been rescued from the power of sin and transferred into the realm of the Beloved. We have both redemption through the blood and forgiveness of our sin. Indeed, this is good news!

Responsive Reading

Leader: Well, brothers and sisters, we have been cold-busted!
People: The God who set a plumb line into our midst has caught us up short.
Leader: The God who judges has called a council meeting and declared that we failed to measure up.
People: We have judged others according to our human standards. We have shown favor to the wealthy and affluent. We have overlooked the poor and the homeless. We have closed our eyes and walked blindly past those begging on the streets.
Leader: They are stumbling, seeking help, and we walk around with our noses in the air.
People: The world is going to hell right in front of our eyes and we are blinded by false gods.
Leader: God created the saints to be gods in the earth! We are created just a little lower than the angels.
People: The Most High depended upon us to lift up the oppressed. The standards were set and we were to surpass, go beyond and above them. We have failed. We need to get up from our stools of doing nothing but talk!
Leader: God seeks those who will go boldly into the world doing acts of justice and being doers of deeds that go beyond even the plumb line in our midst.
People: We ask God for another chance to pass the test of being permanent, positive blessings in the world! We can do it! We will make a difference!

Offertory Invitation

God has promised never to pass us by. With this certainty that all of our needs are met by divine providence we can be generous in our sharing with others who may not even know Jesus Christ. The standard of giving was set by Jesus, who gave his life. What will we render as thanks?

Offertory Praise

God, we have comprehended your grace in Jesus Christ. Now we make attempts to be faithful ministers on his behalf. Let these gifts be acceptable in your sight, we pray, in the name of him who gave his life for us.

Benediction

Leader: Go into the world as the Good Samaritan!
People: We leave to look beyond our immediate sight to be a blessing in the world.
Leader: Go into the world and act differently than the priest who walked by one in need.
People: We go, mindful that we must live the lives we have sung about in godly songs.
Leader: God the High Benchmark; Christ the Criteria Setter; and the Holy Spirit, our Gauge, go before us.
People: Hallelujah and amen.

PROPER 11 · SUNDAY BETWEEN JULY 17 AND JULY 23

Amos 8:1–12 or Genesis 18:1–10a
Psalm 52 or Psalm 15
Colossians 1:15–28
Luke 10:38–42

Call to Worship

Leader: All the hungry people are invited to come to the feast.
People: The table is spread and the feast of God is going on.
Leader: There is a famine in the land.
People: It is not a famine of bread, or a thirst for water, but of hearing the Word of God.
Leader: People have wandered from sea to sea and from north to south.
People: We are here to feast and to worship the Bread of Life.

Call to Confession

Jesus Christ is before all things, and in him all things hold together. He is the head of the body, the Church; he is the beginning, the firstborn from the dead, so that he might have first place in everything. We have allowed other things to take first place in our lives; we need this confession.

Confession

God, in Jesus Christ all the fullness of your divinity and glory was pleased to dwell. And it's through Jesus that we are reconciled to you. We have sinned and ask your forgiveness, by the power of the blood of the Lamb.

Words of Assurance

We, who were once estranged and hostile in mind, doing evil deeds, Jesus has now reconciled in his fleshly body through death, so as to present us holy and blameless and irreproachable before him. This is certainly good news.

Responsive Reading

Leader: Lies! Lies! Lies! There is an abundance of social lies!
People: With smiling faces, lying lips, and honey dripping from their tongues, the leaders of nations speak lies.

Leader: Welfare programs to improve the lives of the poor. Lies!
People: Housing programs to promote the nuclear family. Lies!
Leader: Mortgage programs to share the wealth of the land. Lies!
People: Diversity programs to level the playing field for all people. Lies!
Leader: Wealthy politicians love evil more than good and prefer to lie rather than speak the truth.
People: Yet the Truth hears every one of their lies. The Truth will make us free. The Truth will overthrow every liar!
Leader: The righteous shall see their downfall and have a hearty laugh!
People: For those who trusted in their wealth and forgot God will receive a great wake-up call! We trust God! We have an eternal thing going on!

Offertory Invitation

As Jesus and his disciples were on their way, they entered a certain village, where a woman named Martha welcomed him into her home. She had a sister named Mary, who sat at Jesus' feet and listened to what he was saying. It was a household of hospitality and communion. Our sharing with others shows that we are the same.

Offertory Praise

God, you showed the prophet Amos the harvest of succulent summer fruit in a basket. The harvest was a gift from your earth, your trees, your rain, and your sun and air. All that we have ultimately comes from you. Receive now these gifts in the name of the All-Sufficient One.

Benediction

Leader: The Mystery that has been hidden throughout the ages and generations but that has now been revealed to the saints is Jesus the Christ.
People: We leave as those who have been called and chosen to make his presence known in all the world.
Leader: Go into the world, among those who don't know him, and proclaim the riches of this Mystery.
People: We leave to proclaim God as the Sovereign, the Christ, and the Holy Spirit. For this we have been called. Hallelujah and amen.

PROPER 12 · SUNDAY BETWEEN JULY 24 AND JULY 30

Hosea 1:2–10 or Genesis 18:20–32
Psalm 85 or Psalm 138
Colossians 2:6–15, (16–19)
Luke 11:1–13

Call to Worship

Leader: The husband of a whore is seeking his bride this morning.
People: We have been held captive to human philosophy, empty deceit, and politically correct tradition. Yet, we don't see ourselves as whores!
Leader: The husband of a whore is seeking to have intimate relationships with his bride this morning.
People: We have come to the place of the marriage, wanting restoration and reconciliation.
Leader: The husband of a whore has found the wandering bride.
People: We come to worship the Bridegroom in spirit and in truth.

Call to Confession

The children of Hosea and Gomer were given significant names by the Almighty. Jezreel meant "punishment is forthcoming." Lo-ruhamah meant "no more pity or mercy from God." And the last child's name, Lo-ammi, meant "no longer the children of God." These are our names without the benefit of confession and repentance. Let us share together the prayer that makes us children of the Most High.

Confession

God, we are Gomer! We continue to seek lovers who are not the spouse of our soul. We continue to wander away from "home." We have sinned. Forgive us. Reclaim us. Restore us to the position of your beloved children, we pray, in the name of the Restorer.

Words of Assurance

As we have therefore received Christ Jesus the Lord, we will continue to live our lives in him, rooted and built up in him and established in the faith, just as we have been taught, abounding in thanksgiving that our sins have been taken away. This is news worth shouting about.

Responsive Reading

Leader: Jesus gave the disciples the model prayer. Let us be reminded of its significance.

People: The Creator, who is in heaven, also dared to come to earth and live in our skins and walk in our shoes. This is a holy God, whose name is worthy of praise.

Leader: The realm of God came to earth with the birth of Jesus, who sent the disciples to declare, "The kingdom is nigh you, even in your mouth."

People: Jesus lived to role model for us, then died and rose again to triumph over death. His rising gives us the same power and victory. Our words bring life when we follow his example.

Leader: God is the source of our supply.

People: Every day is a day of anticipation, expectation, receiving of good gifts, and giving thanksgiving for the vast store of blessings that come our way.

Leader: Forgiveness from God is ours as long as we confess, repent, and then forgive others.

People: Too often we block our own blessings. For we honestly don't believe that our unforgiveness of others keeps God from forgiving us! What fools we tend to be in our ignorance.

Leader: The gift of the indwelling Holy Spirit leads us into all paths of truth, keeping us from falling into the multiple temptations before us.

People: To receive this gift of the indwelling, take-control presence of God, all we have to do is ask, "Spirit of the living God, fall afresh on me!" It's just this simple.

Leader: The whole earth belongs to us and we are made from the earth.

People: Surely God's steadfast love and faithfulness will meet. Righteousness and peace will kiss each other. Faithful living reigns from above as the God of the whole earth gives us what is good and we become a fruitful harvest as God's increase.

Offertory Invitation

Jesus taught his followers to ask God for each day's supply of bread. He promised, "For everyone who asks receives, and everyone who searches finds, and for everyone who knocks, the door will be opened." We are often the means to others' prayers for daily bread. Let's us give because we have received.

Offertory Praise

God, when our children ask of us, we give. How grateful we are that when we have asked of you, the precious gift of the Holy Spirit has been given to rule in our hearts. Your realm is now in our hearts. Receive the gifts of your servants, we pray, in the name of Abundant Love.

Benediction

Leader: You have come to fullness and completeness in Jesus Christ, who is the head of every ruler and every authority. Go now into the world with that assurance.

People: In Jesus Christ we have been given a spiritual circumcision and have been baptized to be raised with him through faith in the power of God. We go into the world with this certainty.

Leader: Now unto God, who has erased the record that stood against us, nailed our sin to the cross, disarmed the rulers and authorities in this world, and given us triumph in the world to come, be power, honor, glory, and dominion in our lives forevermore!

People: It is so. Amen!

PROPER 13 · SUNDAY BETWEEN JULY 31 AND AUGUST 6

Hosea 11:1–11 or Ecclesiastes 1:2, 12–14, 2:8–23
Psalm 107:1–9, 43
Colossians 3:1–11
Luke 12:13–21

Call to Worship

Leader: The God who loves us like a mother calls us with tender love.
People: The more God calls, the farther we have moved from this gentle love.
Leader: The God who taught us to walk in paths of righteousness longs to gather us in everlasting arms.
People: We have offered our love to idols and offered our affection to untrustworthy gods.
Leader: The God who leads us with cords of kindness and bands of love, lifts us like infants from our places of shame.
People: We come, like trembling, hardheaded children, to the One Who Love Us Best, with awe, thanksgiving, worship, and praise.

Call to Confession

We are humans with the tendency to go our own way and refuse to heed the wise counsel of the Maker of the Day. We continue to turn away from Love. It is to the detriment of our own soul. This is our time for confession.

Confession

Loving God, as your children we come back home with our heads hanging down. For we have done evil in your sight and forsaken the ways of righteousness. Sin is in us. Like children of Hosea and Gomer, we have no right to approach you on our own. But, through the blessed blood of Christ, our Redeemer, we come asking forgiveness and restoration to our rightful place in your realm.

Words of Assurance

God's promise with our confession is not to execute fierce anger nor destroy us because of our sin. The Holy One returns to us in power and might. And this is good news.

Responsive Reading

Leader: Thanksgiving is due the God who is good and keeps steadfast love for us.

People: We are those who know what it is to be bought back from slavery.

Leader: The diaspora has dispatched us all over the known world.

People: We have had some difficult days and bad situations to face, and God has never forgotten us nor left us without resources.

Leader: Hunger, thirst, and overwhelming pain have faced us, but we have not been destroyed!

People: We have tried serving the gods of the powerful and in-charge. Their gods have not served us well at all. We have divine favor with the God who accompanied our ancestors from Africa.

Leader: From homelessness, namelessness, and landlessness, we have been brought to places never imagined by our foreparents.

People: When we think about the many dangers, toils, and snares that God has preserved us from, there is no way that our souls cannot give out great shouts of thanks!

Leader: For it is by the loving kindness of God that the thirsty are satisfied and the hungry are filled with an assortment of good things.

People: God, give us liberal wisdom to always consider your steadfast love toward us all the days of this life and in the world to come.

Offertory Invitation

So, since we have been raised with Christ, seek the things that are above, where Christ is seated at the right hand of God. We set our minds on things that are above, not on things that are on earth, for we have died and our life is hidden with Christ in God. With thankful hearts we give our temporal offerings in response to this great gift.

Offertory Praise

Jesus Christ, you warned us to "Take care! Be on guard against all kinds of greed; for one's life does not consist in the abundance of things." Things are not are as important as giving to be in line with your will, your way, and your Words of Life. Receive these gifts offered in gratitude for all you have done for us.

Benediction

Leader: Go into the world being rid of anger, wrath, malice, slander, and abusive language.

People: We leave with the wisdom of God that will keep us from lying to one another.

Leader: Go, with the confidence that the old you is buried in Christ.

People: We leave with the full knowledge of being renewed in the image of the Creator.

Leader: Go into the world assured that God the Creator, Jesus the Teacher, and the Holy Spirit, our keeper, give us abundant power!

People: Hallelujah and amen.

PROPER 14 · SUNDAY BETWEEN AUGUST 7 AND AUGUST 13

Isaiah 1:1 or Genesis 15:1–6, 10–20
Psalm 50:1–8, 22–23 or Psalm 33:12–22
Hebrews 11:1–3, 8–16
Luke 12:32–40

Call to Worship

Leader: The God who called an old man, Abraham, and an old, barren woman, Sarah, and used them, calls us today.

People: We come with our failures and our faults, knowing that God will use even us.

Leader: The God who acknowledges our faith as righteousness is seeking those who will step out and follow directions.

People: We come with "now faith," which is the assurance of things hoped for, the conviction of things not seen. Indeed, by faith our ancestors received approval. By faith we understand that the worlds were prepared by the word of God, so that what is seen was made from things that are not visible. We gather to give glory to God with praise and worship.

Call to Confession

God hates our solemn assemblies when sin is present among us. Our festivals, teas, special days, and activities become burdensome to God without holy living. When we stretch out our hands, God will not answer, for there is blood on our hands. We are called to wash ourselves, make ourselves clean, remove the evil of our doings from before our eyes, cease to do evil, learn to do good, seek justice, rescue the oppressed, defend the orphan, and plead for the widow. It seems that we have work and confession set before us. Let us pray.

Confession

Great Architect and Builder, we stand empty before you in our sin. There is nothing good within us and our tendencies to follow our own ways have led us into a mess. We are guilty of not doing what you have commanded. We ask your forgiveness for the sin in our life. We come in faith, that the name of Jesus will wash away our guilt and stain of sin.

Words of Assurance

Come now, says God, let us reason together. Though our sins are like scarlet, they shall be like snow. Though they are red like crimson, they shall become like wool. If we are willing and obedient, we shall eat the good of the land. But if we refuse and rebel, we shall be devoured by the sword, for the mouth of God has spoken. This is good news.

Responsive Reading

Leader: People of God, here comes the Judge.

People: We are summoned by the Maker of the sun and the Creator of the night's light, the stars and the moon.

Leader: The bright dazzle and steady twinkles declare the presence of the Almighty.

People: God always makes an entrance with zestful delight.

Leader: The heavenly elements attest to this call of God for our appearance in God's court.

People: We are the ones who swore on an oath that we would wholeheartedly follow God.

Leader: We have made public declarations that we were sold out for God.

People: Now God has called a meeting to show how far we have fallen by our lives!

Leader: God has kept covenant with us. We have broken the covenant we made with God.

People: We have made public shows of sacrifice, but our hearts were not clean.

Leader: God hates public displays that are empty of meaning and authentic sacrifice.

People: We often serve God only in form and for fashion.

Leader: Mark this! Take good note! Fooling with God will get us blown away.

People: There is no one to deliver us from the wrath of God. We will offer proper praise and thanksgiving with serious holy living to back up our talk!

Offertory Invitation

Do not be afraid, little flock, for it is God's good pleasure to give us the whole realm. We are to sell what we have and give alms to the poor. We are to make purses for ourselves that do not wear out, placing an unfailing treasure in heaven where no thief comes near and no moth can destroy it. For where our treasures are, there our hearts are also. Giving shows where our hearts are located.

Offertory Praise

God, you have promised that those who bring thanksgiving as their sacrifice honor you, and to those who go the right way, you will show the salvation of God. We come with grateful hearts and offer you our gifts. Receive these, we pray, in the name of the Christ.

Benediction

Leader: Leave; be dressed for action and have your lamps lit; be like those who are waiting for the Bridegroom to return from the wedding banquet, so that we may open the door and welcome him when he knocks.
People: We leave to walk worthy of the name Christian, wanting to be ready when the Son of God appears.
Leader: And the world will know that you are Christ-like by your lives. God the Builder, Jesus the Foundation, and the Holy Spirit, the walk-alongside God, go before us.
People: Hallelujah and amen.

PROPER 15 · SUNDAY BETWEEN AUGUST 14 AND AUGUST 20

Isaiah 5:1–7 or Jeremiah 23:23–29
Psalm 80:1–2, 8–19 or Psalm 82
Hebrews 11:29–12:2
Luke 12:49–56

Call to Worship

Leader: The Creator of the Garden is looking for ripe vines as a blessing of growth and grace!
People: We are the Beloved's well-tended offspring.
Leader: The Watcher in the Tower is anticipating the sweetness of grapes.
People: The Vine Dresser has called and we are here to answer with songs of joyful praise.

Call to Confession

The One who dug the garden and cleared it of stones, the One who planted choice vines and placed a watchtower in the midst, has dug out a wine vat expecting the harvest of good grapes. What we bring as a crop is failure to produce. This is our time of confession.

Confession

Gracious God, there is no more that you could have done to receive a decent harvest. The fault lies within us. You are well within your rights to remove our hedge of protection, to allow our walls of defense to be destroyed and our lives trampled. However, we admit our sin. We ask for your forgiveness in the name of the Vine of Life.

Words of Assurance

The vineyard of the God of Hosts is the house of Israel, and the people of Judah are pleasant planting. Our confession brings about clouds of rain to provide for our continuance in God's favor. This is good news.

Responsive Reading

Leader: The Master Planter has delivered the vine from slavery in Egypt.

People: The Church of the Living God has been transplanted from dirges to melodies of delight.

Leader: God provided good, black earth and filled the garden with sunshine and rain.

People: The vine took root way down and began to grow up and out.

Leader: From sea to shining sea, from mountain top to valley low, from desert plains to succulent earth the vine has climbed and crept.

People: God took good care of the vine. The vine began to run and to grow wild. God stepped back.

Leader: The hedges were trampled, the protection was removed, the wild animals begin to eat the vine.

People: God knew all the time that the vine needed tending. God wanted the vine to notice its own neglect!

Leader: The wild growing vine lost its healthy appeal.

People: The God of gardens, plowed fields, and neglected grounds turned and saw the shape of the vine.

Leader: The poor vine had almost died. Pruning, cutting, hoeing, and chopping were necessary for the future life of the vine.

People: The fires of adversity made the vine glad to be revived although it was greatly cut back.

Leader: The strong hand of God was once again placed upon the growth of the vine.

People: The vine is preserved for God's name sake. God's reputation is on the line. The vine must make the Vine Owner look good! Restore us, O God. Let your face smile upon us with favor again. We want to be saved.

Offertory Invitation

We are called to pray in the Spirit at all times in every prayer and supplication. And we are to keep alert and to always persevere in intercessions for all the people of God. Our giving is a glorious intercession.

Offertory Praise

Therefore, since we are surrounded by so great a cloud of witnesses, let us also lay aside every weight and the sin that clings so closely, and let us run with perseverance the race that is set before us, looking to Jesus, the pioneer and perfecter of our faith, who for the sake of the joy that was set before him endured the cross, disregarding its shame, and has taken his seat at the right hand of the throne of God. We pray in the name of the Vine of Life.

Benediction

Leader: Finally, go and be strong in the Lord and in the strength of God's power.

People: We have put on the whole armor of God that we may be able to stand against the tricks of the devil.

Leader: Our struggles are not against those of flesh and blood, but against the ruler of this present world.

People: We will stand!

Leader: And, having done all you know, stand! God the Truth, Jesus Christ the Righteous, and the Strength of the Holy Spirit undergird us!

People: Hallelujah and amen.

PROPER 16 · SUNDAY BETWEEN AUGUST 21 AND AUGUST 27

Jeremiah 1:4–10 or Isaiah 58:9b–14
Psalm 71:1–6 or Psalm 103:1–8
Hebrews 12:18–29
Luke 13:10–17

Call to Worship

Leader: Come to the Mountain and meet the blazing fire.
People: The sound of the trumpet has been clear in its summons.
Leader: The Voice whose words makes the audience beg is present to speak.
People: We have come to Mt. Zion, the city of the Living God, with sacrifices of praise.
Leader: The Yet Once More is present to disturb us.
People: We are receiving a realm that cannot be shaken; let us give thanks, by which we offer to God an acceptable worship with reverence and awe; for indeed our God is a consuming fire.

Call to Confession

There is an assembly of the firstborn who are enrolled in heaven, where God is the judge of all. The spirits of the righteous made perfect are there, and so is Jesus Christ, the mediator of the New Covenant. To ensure that our space there is reserved, let us offer confession with contrite hearts.

Confession

Yet Once More, it is we who return again with confession upon our lips and repentance in our hearts. We tried so diligently not to fail you and to mess up this past week. But we failed. Our human tendencies got in the way and we have sinned. Forgive us. Restore our souls to a place of health in you, we pray in the name of the Lamb, who takes our sin away.

Words of Assurance

Today we are appointed over nations and over kingdoms, to pluck up and to pull down, to destroy and to overthrow, to build and to plant. It is an awesome assignment. The good news is that God empowers us to just do it. Thanks be to God.

Responsive Reading

Leader: God knew us before we were formed in our mothers' bellies.
People: Our assignments were given and our consecrations were assured.
Leader: There is no excuse for failing to carry out our missions.
People: The Almighty God has equipped us from before birth and attends to us daily.
Leader: Childhood, middle age, and later years are not excuses to be used before God.
People: Our God is a rock of refuge, a strong sanctuary, and a sure defense from all odds.
Leader: In our childhood the God in us showed us the way for our path to be directed.
People: Our hope has never been in our own strength, but in the power of the God who called us before our forming.
Leader: God has great expectations of us. With our speech we create God's world.
People: Your hands are upon us, Great God, and our lips will speak forth your Words of Life. Incline yourself to us, once more and again.

Offertory Invitation

Yet once more we have an opportunity to evidence our lip service by our deeds. Let us be liberal givers since the God we serve has been so generous towards us.

Offertory Praise

God, innumerable angels bow before you today in the festal gathering. They sing forth your power, praise, and majesty throughout the heavens. Please receive these our offerings that your name might be spread throughout the earth. We give them in the name of our Hope.

Benediction

Leader: The God who sees us sends us back into the world.
People: The God who calls us has spoken encouraging words for us to take on our way.

Leader: The God who touches us and empowers us also goes before us to light our path.

People: The God who frees us to free others is awaiting our ministry beyond these walls.

Leader: The bent-over woman did not leave the same way she came into the temple.

People: We, too, have been freed from our ailments and delivered from our excuses. We stand prepared to be God's agents of change in the world.

Leader: May the God who formed us, the Christ who paid for our redemption, and the Holy Spirit who transforms us day by day keep us til we meet again.

People: Hallelujah and amen!

PROPER 17 · SUNDAY BETWEEN AUGUST 28 AND SEPTEMBER 3

Jeremiah 2:4–13 or Proverbs 25:6–7
Psalm 81:1, 10–16 or Psalm 112
Hebrews 13:1–8, 15–16
Luke 14:1, 7–14

Call to Worship

Leader: The One who speaks harsh words calls us this day.
People: Too often we take kind words as weakness and soft words as permission to do our own thing.
Leader: The God who challenges our turning away summons us this day.
People: The way of life is so difficult. We have sinned but we have some excellent excuses!
Leader: God has heard all of our excuses and will not accept any of them.
People: We have come to worship and to be made right with our God.

Call to Confession

Hear the Word of the Lord, people of God. God asks, what did our ancestors find so wrong with the providence of the Holy One that they would go in search of worthless things and make gods of them? Without a doubt, we continue their straying-away-from-God pattern. God's wrath was loosed on them. To avoid these severe consequences, confession is demanded of us.

Confession

God, you have brought us such a mighty long way. You have delivered us from the captivity of slavery and brought many of us to positions of influence and power. You continue to provide for us and our families. Yet we have made our godly heritage an abomination by the multiple ways we disregard your path. We have sinned. We have done things that have profited us nothing. Restore us again, we pray, in the name of the Bread of Life.

Words of Assurance

Love always reaches out to us. Grace always restores us. And the Living Water will quench our thirst for the meaninglessness that leads us astray. This is good news.

Responsive Reading

Leader: Submission is the word of the day.

People: We are those who like to have it our way.

Leader: Submission is the way of holy living.

People: We want to live holy and we want to be part of the in-crowd, too.

Leader: Submission has great benefits that willful living won't provide.

People: God has shown us strength, majesty, and power that we couldn't even imagine.

Leader: God's love is proven, time and time again, when we submit to the way established for us.

People: Our stubborn hearts have led us to follow our own counsel. We really do believe that we have it pretty much together.

Leader: What has our way earned us? What enemies have we defeated on our own? What political structures have we overturned with our human strength?

People: Submission is the word of the day. Submission is the way of holy living. Submission wins for us the entire providence of the One who made and maintains the heavens and the earth. We pray for the grace to submit to the better way of God.

Offertory Invitation

Through Jesus Christ, let us continually offer a sacrifice of praise to God. The fruit of our lips is praise that extols the worth of God's majestic name. We are challenged not to neglect to do what is good and to share what we have, for such sacrifices are pleasing to God. It's giving time.

Offertory Praise

God, we are making every attempt to become free from the love of money and to be content with what you provide. For your promise is that you will never leave us nor forsake us, so that as we give we also say with the saints of the ages, "The Lord is our helper, we will not be afraid, for what can anyone do to us?" We pray that you receive our gifts in the name of the One who holds yesterday, today, and forevermore.

Benediction

Leader: Go into the world, letting mutual love continue.

People: We leave to be hospitable to strangers, knowing that we will encounter angels along our way during the week.

Leader: Go into the world, remembering those in institutions.

People: We leave to do the greater works of Jesus Christ as we touch the world.

Leader: The Dominion, the Truth, and the Power go before us!

People: Hallelujah and amen.

PROPER 18 · SUNDAY BETWEEN SEPTEMBER 4 AND SEPTEMBER 10

Jeremiah 18:1–11 or Deuteronomy 30:15–20
Psalm 139:1–6, 13–18 or Psalm 1
Philemon 1–21
Luke 14:25–33

Call to Worship

Leader: The God of broken vessels calls together all cracked pots.
People: The Potter wants to make us over again.
Leader: The God who longs to put us back together again is in the house this morning.
People: We gather at the Potter's house for mending, making, and remaking. Glory to the Worthy Potter.

Call to Confession

God told Jeremiah, the prophet, to watch the pot-throwing process. Jeremiah was shocked to see that God was a potter shaping evil against the children of Israel and devising a plan against them. However, God gave them and us a way out. "Turn now, all of you, from your evil way, and amend your ways and your doings." This is our call to confession.

Confession

God, surely we are cracked pots. We have leaked all over people and places this past week. Some of the stuff we leaked was not worthy of being placed into the world. Some of the stuff we leaked, we needed for our own preservation. But cracked pots cannot heal themselves. Remember us today, we pray. For we are sinners in need of your grace and mercy. Fix us. Fill us. Use us, we pray, in the name of the Potter's Glue, Jesus the Christ.

Words of Assurance

God reworks cracked pots, mends them in loving care, and uses them to bring glory and honor to the Name above All Names. Thanks be to God.

Responsive Reading

Leader: The investigating God is on the case.

People: Our hidden lives are just like open books before the Light.

Leader: We cannot outdistance ourselves from God.

People: God knows us from the inside out, and that's really up close and personal.

Leader: Before we can form a lie on our tongue, God is aware!

People: The night and the day, the time gone by and the time to come, are alike to the All-Knowing God.

Leader: The mighty hand of God is upon our very lives.

People: There is no spot where God is not! What wonderful assurance for our lives.

Leader: God formed us with precision in our mothers' wombs.

People: It was God who decided to whom we would be born at the proper time.

Leader: God had designed great plans for our lives before we were created by egg and sperm!

People: God covers us with great grace and amazing shalom! We are awfully special to God and each one is a divine design.

Leader: It's totally incomprehensible that we are never out of the thoughts of God!

People: How vast are the thoughts of God toward us individually and corporately. If we would make attempts to number them, it would be like trying to count all the grains of sands! Before we began and when our earthly day ends, we are encompassed by the love of God.

Offertory Invitation

The Apostle Paul prayed that the sharing of our faith would become effective as we perceive all the good that we may do for Christ. People that we will never see, touch, or know are blessed when we share in our love for the whole people of God.

Offertory Praise

Jesus Christ declared that we could not become disciples if we did not give up all of our possessions. God, we want to be disciples. Receive these, our gifts, in his great name, we pray.

Benediction

Leader: Go, counting the cost of discipleship.

People: We will pick up our crosses and follow Jesus Christ.

Leader: Go, making sure to finish whatever you start.

People: Deeds triumph over words.

Leader: Go, being generous with your forgiveness.

People: God so loved us that Jesus came to restore us.

Leader: God the Potter, Jesus Christ the Pure Vessel, and the Holy Spirit, the Vessel Perfecter, work in us both the will and the ability to do every good work.

People: Hallelujah and amen.

PROPER 19 · SUNDAY BETWEEN SEPTEMBER 11 AND SEPTEMBER 17

Jeremiah 4:11–12, 22–28 or Exodus 32:7–14
Psalm 14 or Psalm 51:1–10
1 Timothy 1:12–17
Luke 15:1–10

Call to Worship

Leader: The God who seeks counsel with stupid children seeks us.
People: The God of skilled evil workers wants to spend time with us.
Leader: God longs for relationship with those who have no understanding.
People: Those who don't have a concept of doing good are sought by the Triune God.
Leader: The Trinity has called for those who are snared in foolishness.
People: We have heard the summons. This is the right place. We have come with gratitude to worship God, who has called us to gather.

Call to Confession

The saying is sure and worthy of full acceptance, that Christ Jesus came into the world to save sinners, of whom we are the foremost. But for this very reason we will receive mercy with our confession and repentance of our sin. Let us pray.

Confession

Calling God, we have heard the joyful sound that Jesus saves. We have been guilty of sin in the week gone by. Violence has reigned in us, acted through us, and been in charge of our physical temples. Forgive us our sin. We plead for your grace and mercy, that we might be in right relationship with you. We pray in the Name Above All Names.

Words of Assurance

With our confession we have received mercy, so that in us, as the prime example, Jesus Christ might display the utmost patience, making us the examples to those who would come to believe in him for eternal life. This is certainly good news.

Responsive Reading

Leader: The world has tried hard to make God disappear.

People: The Church has made every attempt to put God in a small and confining box.

Leader: Denominations have tried to make God their personal puppet.

People: Even we want God to become our instant bellhop, who disappears when our troubles are gone.

Leader: Could it be possible that we believe that God is bound by our will, our ways, and our traditions?

People: The God of Intellect seeks those who are not completely stupid!

Leader: God's roaming eye searches high and low for the very few who realize the sovereignty of the One who made the beginning.

People: The Holy One is coming up short! We are not being elected to represent God by our lives!

Leader: God is sick of us perpetrating! God is weary of our play acting! God is fed up with our playing Church!

People: God is seeking leaders for a sick people.

Leader: God's patience has worn thin with leaders who are serving up junk-food meals to hungry people.

People: God's reserve nerve has been pushed with leaders too busy to pray.

Leader: We cannot trifle with the last, the least, and the seemingly insignificant. These are God's primary concern.

People: Payday is coming soon. We will get paid according to our work for God.

Leader: Oh, that deliverance would come from us who are the so-called "Church."

People: Oh, that we might become the Church by the living of our talk! This would make God so glad and change the wages we are earning to eternal life and joy.

Offertory Invitation

God has such a special affinity for the poor. The judgment of God, like a hot wind from the bare heights of the barren desert, is upon all those of us who withhold from sharing. That we might not be judged as greedy or stingy, let us share from what we have received. For all that we have is a gift from a generous God.

Offertory Praise

Judge of Every Deed, we offer these gifts so that the desert might be a fruitful place and cities might be spared from desolation and ruin. We want to share so that others might come into your mighty realm and we can rejoice with the angelic host, worshiping the One who saves to the uttermost. It's in his name that we pray.

Benediction

Leader: Leave in faith, looking unto the Ruler of the ages, immortal and invisible. To the only God be honor and glory forever.
People: Hallelujah and amen.

PROPER 20 · SUNDAY BETWEEN SEPTEMBER 18 AND SEPTEMBER 24

Jeremiah 8:18–9:1 or Amos 8:4–7
Psalm 79:1–9 or Psalm 113
1 Timothy 2:1–7
Luke 16:1–13

Call to Worship

Leader: First of all, we are urged to beseech God with prayers, intercessions, and thanksgiving for everyone.
People: We are present for worship, remembering our assignment.
Leader: We are to pray for leadership everywhere, so that we may live peaceful lives with dignity.
People: This is right and acceptable in the sight of God, our Savior.
Leader: God desires that the whole world be saved and come to the knowledge of the Truth.
People: For there is one God and one mediator between God and humankind, Christ Jesus.
Leader: Jesus slipped into our skin, walked in our shoes, and gave himself as our ransom for sin.
People: We have come to know Jesus in the pardon of our sin. We have accepted the Great Commission. And we have come to worship that we might go out and be the Church in the world.

Call to Confession

We are called to give God an accounting of the ways in which we have managed our lives this past week. The record against us does not look good. Thank God for a period of confession so that the sin we have committed might be washed away. Let us pray.

Confession

Help us, O God of our salvation, for the glory of your name. Deliver us. And forgive us our sin for the sake of your righteous name, we pray in the name of Christ.

Words of Assurance

The atoning blood of Jesus is ours to cover our sins. With confession and repentance they are thrown into the Sea of Forgetfulness. God will not remember them again. Let us not repeat them, by the power of the Holy Spirit given unto us as leader and guide. This is our good news.

Responsive Reading

Leader: Sometimes it seems as if we have been forsaken by God.
People: Say that! Our joy is gone. Grief is upon us. Our hearts are sick when we see our nation, our people, and our communities.
Leader: It seems that the violence between us has become worse than what the enemy used on us.
People: We continue to live out of the great scheme that pitted us against each other.
Leader: But we have to realize that it is a trick of the enemy when we see us killing us!
People: The world laughs at us. We are too often a joke to the world. We are on the very bottom of everyone's list. How long will God be angry with us?
Leader: You would think that God would punish those who have no consideration of the worth of the things of God.
People: Instead it appears that we are even being punished by the Almighty. When will it be our turn?
Leader: Let us pray that the ancestors' sins are not ours. Let us pray that the compassion of God comes speedily to meet us, for we are in difficult times and in a difficult spot between a rock and a hard place.
People: We carry the name of God. For the sake of the Most High's name, we pray for a speedy deliverance, that desolation might not be our end.

Offertory Invitation

No slave can serve two masters; for a slave will either hate the one and love the other, or be devoted to the one and despise the other. We are slaves for Christ. We cannot serve God and wealth. For the sake of Christ, let us share the wealth we have.

Offertory Praise

God, we are ready to move into more gracious living. Therefore, we have given as unto you. We want you to entrust us with all true riches—that is, abundant life now and, then, life eternal. We give in the name of the One who paid our bill with you in full.

Benediction

Leader: Remember this week, do not squander the properties of the Master.

People: We leave to do the right things in the name of the Christ.

Leader: Remember this week to be as wise as serpents but as gentle as doves.

People: We leave to be faithful to the name by which we identify ourselves, children of God.

Leader: God, the Chief Physician; Jesus Christ, the Balm of Gilead; and the Holy Spirit, the Restorer, go with us and before us. Go in peace!

People: Hallelujah and amen.

PROPER 21 · SUNDAY BETWEEN SEPTEMBER 25 AND OCTOBER 1

Jeremiah 32:1–3a, 6–15 or Amos 6:1a, 4–7
Psalm 91:1–6 or Psalm 146, 14–16
1 Timothy 6:6–19
Luke 16:19–31

Call to Worship

Leader: The Lord of Hosts, the God of Israel, says to make serious our election.
People: We have come to serve the God of houses and lands.
Leader: The God who provides redemption comes with terms of investment.
People: We gather in the presence of witnesses to declare the One Born to Die.
Leader: There are conditions, regulations, and agreements necessary to be followers.
People: Our call and election is sure. We come to worship our refuge, our fortress, and our God.

Call to Confession

God's Only Begotten Son was born to cover us with his pinions and offer his wings for our fortress from the storms of life. He came to deliver us from the snare of every deadly pestilence so that we would not have to fear the terror of the night or the weapons of the day. Neither pestilence that stalks in the night nor the destruction that awaits us at noonday can come near us when we are hidden in the shelter of the Most High. As we have moved away in this past week, let us pray.

Confession

Demanding Presence, we are drawn into your presence by your love. And we find ourselves to be unworthy to even stand before you. Our sin separates us. Forgive us. Let mercy be the bridge that restores us to the shelter we need in you. Forgive us. Save us from ourselves, we pray in the name of the One who died in our place.

Words of Assurance

Those who love God are delivered. Those who obey God are protected by that great name. When we call, God has promised to answer us. With long life we will be satisfied and God will reveal unto us the gift of salvation. This is the promise of the Promise Keeper God.

Responsive Reading

Leader: In El Shaddai's presence is where we long to be.
People: The God who always provides has a safe house for those of us who believe, trust, and are faithful to our covenant commitments.
Leader: Linger in the presence of God. Worship at all times. Use words when necessary.
People: Praise, thanksgivings, petitions, confessions, adoration, and love songs keep us on God's mind.
Leader: Lean on the Everlasting Arms. All is well.
People: We have nothing to fear or be afraid of when in the presence of the Ancient of Days.
Leader: No wild beasts, creatures, or humans can steal us from God's protection.
People: Night or day makes no difference to the All-Seeing Eye.
Leader: Those on our right and left might fall out and be conquered.
People: We stand safe and secure from all alarms.
Leader: Fear not, for there is great joy.
People: The angelic host are on notice to guard us in all of our ways. Even when we stumble, slip, and fall down, the help of heaven is there to steady our feeble steps. We are holding onto the unchanging hand of God for dear life. For the end of the story is that God has promised protection, long life here, and everlasting life on the other side. What a time that will be!

Offertory Invitation

Houses, fields, and vineyards are all part of God's promise to a landless people without any political affiliation or significance. God made the covenant and honored it. We have entered into covenant with God. Now is the time when we do in small measure what we have promised to do to ensure that all might live in abundance. Let's give.

Offertory Praise

God, the rich man, lavishly dressed, lived the "good" life and awoke in hell. The beggar, in rags, often had no food and was shown little hospitality, even by the one who had more than enough to share. He awoke, on the other side of time, in your arms. The rich man begged that we would come to a place of not wanting to end up in his place of torment, and we don't. We have given to help the world, especially the poor beggars who have nothing. Please accept our gifts in the name of your child, Jesus Christ.

Benediction

Leader: Go, keep the commandments! Realize there is great gain in godliness combined with contentment.

People: We leave, understanding that we brought nothing into the world and can take nothing out of it.

Leader: Go, remembering that the love of money is the root of all kinds of evil, and those who want to be rich fall into temptation and are trapped by many senseless and harmful desires that plunge people into ruin and destruction.

People: We leave to pursue righteousness, godliness, faith, love, endurance, and gentleness. We will fight the good fight of faith.

Leader: Go, being examples of the great and blessed Sovereign, King of Kings and Lord of Lords. He alone has immortality and dwells in the unapproachable light. To him be honor and eternal dominion.

People: Hallelujah and amen.

PROPER 22 · SUNDAY BETWEEN OCTOBER 2 AND OCTOBER 8

Lamentations 1:1–6 or Habakkuk 1:1–4, 2:1–4
Psalm 137 or Psalm 37:1–9
2 Timothy 1:1–14
Luke 17:5–10

Call to Worship

Leader: By the great Mississippi River we were set down, and there we wept when we remembered Mother Africa.
People: On the weeping willows we hung our calling drums.
Leader: Slave masters mocked us and told us to sing merry songs.
People: How could we raise our voices in merriment while suffering in an unfriendly land?
Leader: If we forget Mother Africa, we erase our roots.
People: If we forget Mother Africa, we wipe out the place of our origin. Let our tongues cleave to the roof of our mouths, let our feet forget to beat, and our hands forget to wave if we ever fail to remember from where God brought us. For the God who has brought us safely this far, we gather to give praise and to sing.

Call to Confession

The days have been long and the way difficult. Many have turned their backs, given up hope, and walked away from God. How many times last week we blew it! Yet we have gathered again this day. This is our time to confess.

Confession

We are mourners in Zion this morning, God. We weep bitterly in the night. So-called friends and associates have failed us and let us down. Our children have wandered away and our family relationships are in turmoil. In our pain, too often we forget you. We have sinned. We have forfeited the majesty you bestowed upon us in the beginning. Forgive us and renew our strength for the journey, we pray in the name of the Lion of the Tribe.

Words of Assurance

We are the people of Christ Jesus by the perfect will of God, for the sake of the promise of life that is in Christ Jesus. This is our good news.

Responsive Reading

Leader: How have we, a nation destined for greatness, fallen away?
People: We have become like a penniless widow.
Leader: We were created with divine design.
People: Now we cry like a woman without a lover.
Leader: Those who claimed to be our friends have walked away.
People: It doesn't feel good to be at the end of the line all the time.
Leader: It feels like we live in a state of exile and suffering.
People: We stay stuck on stupid, spinning in our own distress.
Leader: God, no one runs to our defense while we suffer lack.
People: Our children have become the captives of the get-rich culture!
Leader: Now our very best, our most educated, and our finest take on Muslim names and are searching for religion.
People: What have we done, God? Or should we ask, what have we left undone? The ball is in our court. God is waiting on our next move!

Offertory Invitation

Through it all, we are not ashamed, for we know the One in whom we have put our trust. We are persuaded that God is more than able! We even trust to share from what we have with those we don't know as we give.

Offertory Praise

God, we are guarding the good treasure entrusted to us by you. With the help of the Holy Spirit, we give in the name of Divine Grace.

Benediction

Leader: If we have faith the size of a mustard seed, we will be able to speak to every mountain in our lives this week.
People: We leave to be mountain movers! .
Leader: Speak to the mountain in faith!
People: Mountain, move out of our way! We stand in the faith of the Authority, the Salvation, and the Power! Hallelujah and amen.

PROPER 23 · SUNDAY BETWEEN OCTOBER 9 AND OCTOBER 15

Jeremiah 29:1, 4–7 or 2 Kings 5:1–3, 7–15c
Psalm 66:1–12 or Psalm 11
2 Timothy 2:8–15
Luke 17:11–19

Call to Worship

Leader: The Investment God is here!
People: We serve the God who invested image, intellect, and breath in us.
Leader: The God who has stock in our humanness and holds interest in our lives has arrived.
People: We have an appointment with Our Broker, who works diligently on our behalf.
Leader: The Accountant of Life holds us responsible for the spending of all of our days.
People: Sovereign God, we have gathered to invest our time, energy, and praise in song and word during this period of worship.

Call to Confession

Christ Jesus was raised from the dead after suffering hardship. We are called as followers to endure everything for the sake of wearing his precious name. This is our portfolio if we hope to attain the salvation that leads to eternal life. For what we have refused to do and that which we have done wrong, this is our time to confess.

Confession

God, the saying is sure: if we have died with Jesus in our baptism we will also live with him in eternity. If we endure hardship as good soldiers, we will also reign with Jesus in glory. If we deny Jesus, he will also deny us. But if we are faithless, Jesus still remains faithful, for he cannot deny himself. We have failed to keep our agreement with you. Our behaviors this past week are not worthy of your investment in us. We have sinned. We will not wrangle over words. Please forgive us so that we may be approved by you, workers with no need to be ashamed, but rightly explaining the Word of Truth, in whose name we dare to pray. Fix us to see your face, we pray in the name of the Redeemer.

Words of Assurance

We can get up, grateful for being healed of our sin. We can go on with the journey we have begun, assured that our faith in the unfailing forgiveness of God has made us well. Certainly this is good news!

Responsive Reading

Leader: Jump for joy as we get ready to call out a shout to be heard all around the world.

People: It's exciting to whoop it up for God. We offer God our sacrifice of praise.

Leader: We can call out "Awesome God" as the real deal for the great deeds God has performed on our behalf.

People: There is no doubt that God is celebrated around the globe, for the deeds of majesty are world renowned.

Leader: Come and see what God has done! Awesome exploits extol the victories of God on behalf of the poor, the oppressed, and the marginalized everywhere.

People: The Deliverer is not isolated to this soil! The Triumphant One has done valiant and bold exhibits of power the world over.

Leader: God rejoices in uprooting rotten leaders and expelling those who steal land not belonging to them.

People: The Eye That Never Slumbers or Sleeps roams the world. The rebellious will not do wrong and get away clean.

Leader: Bless our God, all people! Let the sound of praise be heard.

People: We bless the name of the Most High God.

Leader: We are yet in the land of the living; the blood is running warm in our veins. We have not been destroyed despite the many plots against us.

People: We have been tested and tried by God. Great burdens have been laid upon us. But God has always been our rock and our strength.

Leader: Others have felt they were our superiors. God allowed us to be made very low.

People: We have gone through the fires of an earthly hell. We should have been dead and gone! But fire did not destroy us nor did we drown in the waters of the Middle Passage. God has brought us this far and today we stand in a wealthy space. We stand firm in our God. You can't beat this!

Offertory Invitation

According to American history, we have been "the lepers"! We have been cast aside, assigned certain ghettoes, and told just how far we could progress. Jesus has given us freedom, liberty, and power. Our giving is one way that we express our gratitude.

Offertory Praise

Jesus, Master, have mercy on us. Too often we fail to say sufficient thanks for the many blessings we receive. In our spirits, like the Samaritan leper, we lay prostrate before you and offer our small gifts for your great grace and healing power. Let other lepers be cleansed and made whole; this is our prayer that we make in your matchless name.

Benediction

Leader: Jesus had the audacity to go into the area where the lepers were contained.
People: Freedom in the Spirit lead him into strange and unorthodox places.
Leader: The Word of Jesus to the begging lepers sent them on a mission.
People: The lepers were healed as they moved out at the command of Jesus.
Leader: Go, in that same fashion. The Great Physician, the Healer, and the Anointing Holy Spirit empower us to be on our way, healing as we go.
People: Hallelujah and amen.

PROPER 24 · SUNDAY BETWEEN OCTOBER 16 AND OCTOBER 22

Jeremiah 31:27–34 or Genesis 32:22–31
Psalm 119:97–104 or Psalm 121
2 Timothy 3:14–4:5
Luke 18:1–8

Call to Worship

Leader: The New Covenant God wants an audience with us.
People: The authentic Attorney General is reigning in this house.
Leader: The Original Lawgiver seeks to write upon our hearts.
People: We open our hearts as we worship and offer our praise.

Call to Confession

No longer do we have to teach each other or say to one another, "Know the Lord." God promised to write the Eternal Covenant upon our hearts. Because we know that we are covenant breakers, let us confess.

Confession

Builder, Planner, and Lawgiver, you have done so much for us until we cannot tell it all. The words fail as we make feeble attempts to give a summary of your interventions in our lives. Yet we have done what is evil in your sight. Forgive us our sin, we ask in the name of your Son, Jesus the Christ.

Words of Assurance

The promise of God is not only forgiveness of our sins; but the amazing thing is that they will not be remembered anymore. We are free of sin!

Responsive Reading

Leader: If we would simply continue in the ways the ancestors taught us we would be so much better.
People: We heard them. We memorized them. We just don't actualize them in our lives the way that we should.
Leader: From childhood we have learned the sacred Scriptures.

People: They have instructed us in the way of salvation.

Leader: The sacred text was inspired by the Ancient of Days.

People: Following that counsel keeps us on the narrow way to eternal life. As we put the words to practice in our lives we become better.

Leader: The Holy Scriptures equip the people of God in doing random acts of kindness.

People: We are urged to proclaim the message of salvation.

Leader: Whether the time is favorable or unfavorable, we have an assignment to carry out.

People: We are to convince, chastise, and encourage others with sincere patience as we teach. For during the times in which we live, many don't want to hear truth, but fairy tales and good-sounding myths.

Leader: What are we to do, people of God?

People: We covenant to be sober, to endure our tests, to do the work of winning souls, and to carry out our assignments completely. No excuse is acceptable. We have much work to do!

Offertory Invitation

Everyone who belongs to God is proficient and equipped for every good work. It's time for sharing in the offering. And we each have something to share for the work of the ministry.

Offertory Praise

God, we are so thankful that you answer prayer. We appreciate the persistent widow, who teaches us to hold on to the horns of the altar until justice belongs to us. Many are doing like her around the world. We are the answer to many of their prayers. Thank you that we can lighten others' burdens. We offer these gifts in the name of our Burden Bearer.

Benediction

Leader: The Unjust Judge is alive and well in the world that we will face.

People: We go into the world with the persistence of the widow.

Leader: Go, encouraged by the promise that God has no respect of person.

People: It is no secret what God can do when we are faithful in prayer.

Leader: God the Answer, Jesus the Great Questioner, and the Holy Spirit keep us strong til we meet again.

People: Hallelujah and amen.

PROPER 25 · SUNDAY BETWEEN OCTOBER 23 AND OCTOBER 29

Joel 2:23–32 or Jeremiah 14:7–10, 19–22
Psalm 65 or Psalm 84:1–7
2 Timothy 4:6–8, 16–18
Luke 18:9–14

Call to Worship

Leader: The God of the harvest is ready to receive praise.
People: For the early, abundant, and later rain, we offer thanksgiving.
Leader: The God who fills the baskets with the finest grains prepares for our homage.
People: For the threshing floors, the vats of wine, and the oil we bow in reverence.
Leader: We can eat and be satisfied. We have not been left to starve.
People: Great is the God who is in our midst, providing for our needs. We come to worship.

Call to Confession

The Holy Spirit has been poured out on all flesh; our sons and our daughters prophesy. Our old men dream dreams, and our young men see visions. Everyone who calls upon the name of God shall be saved. God has made a way of escape for each of us. Confession opens the way for us to be filled with God's spirit. This is our call to confession.

Confession

God, like Paul, we want to say that we have fought the good fight, finished our course, and kept the faith. That's what we want to say. The real deal is that we run from fights, don't finish what we start, and forget our faith on down days. And you know this already. So, without pretense, we come to confess our sin. For we know that you are the righteous judge and that there can be a crown of righteousness laid up for us if we live according to your will. Forgive us. Restore us. Use us, we pray, in the name of your darling son, Jesus.

Words of Assurance

The Sovereign God will rescue us from every evil attack and save us for the eternal realm. To the All Wise God we give glory forever and ever. This is good news.

Responsive Reading

Leader: The time has come to offer the sacrifice of praise.
People: Often our praise is silent, for words are not adequate to express our thanks to God.
Leader: We serve the God who both initiated and answers prayer.
People: In the cool of the evening God came seeking Adam and Eve, who in their hiding were actually praying for grace and mercy.
Leader: Their sin of rebellion and disobedience was overwhelming to them.
People: While they were hiding and afraid, God came seeking them with the plan for salvation and restoration.
Leader: With the coming of God's Son we have the privilege to return to the Sanctuary in confidence.
People: Our God is an awesome wonder who delivered us before we could dare ask.
Leader: God planned the earth and all that is in it as a birthday present to the rebellious humans.
People: The waters were separated, the mountains were planted, the oceans, seas, and lakes were given their boundaries. Animals were created and winged animals began to fly. Mother Earth was made to reproduce and God provided dew to encourage growth.
Leader: Harvest was planned before the first crop was spoken into being!
People: For the End created the Beginning! Every year the bounty of God is our yield. Our daily intake was in God's mind, and it was an overflowing scheme of harvest.
Leader: The pastures of the earth continue to overflow. The hills deck themselves with floral joy.
People: The lush meadows clothe themselves and the valleys offer us their grain. The harvest is simply nature's way of offering praise unto our generous God. We come along in harmony.

Offertory Invitation

Dawn and dusk each have a special show that they put on for the Creator. They know who made them and empowered them to last through the ages. The waters flow in mysterious patterns, gurgling their delight unto God. The fields bloom in generosity. From the harvest that we have received, let us prepare to tell God "Thanks."

Offertory Praise

God, you visit the earth and water it. You greatly enrich it for our abundance. Our storehouses overflow with your richness as the earth gives us its bounty. We are grateful recipients and offer our gifts as a token of our unpayable debt. We pray in the name of the Christ.

Benediction

Leader: Go, trusting in the God who never fails.
People: Jesus, Son of David, have mercy on us.
Leader: Go, understanding that God longs to answer our prayers.
People: Jesus, Son of David, have mercy on us.
Leader: Go, realizing that without a dependence upon God, we cannot make it.
People: Jesus, Son of David, have mercy on us.
Leader: Go in peace! Our humble stance before God will carry us through.
People: Hallelujah and amen.

PROPER 26 · SUNDAY BETWEEN OCTOBER 30 AND NOVEMBER 5

Habakkuk 1:1–4, 2:1–4 or Isaiah 1:10–18
Psalm 119:137–144 or Psalm 32:1–7
2 Thessalonians 1:1–4, 11–12
Luke 19:1–10

Call to Worship

Leader: To the Church of God gathered in this house, grace to you and peace be multiplied.
People: We have gathered to give thanks to God for the privilege of brothers and sisters.
Leader: This is right because our faith is growing in abundance.
People: And our love for one another is increasing. We boast in God.
Leader: The scattered Church has been steadfast and faithful during our times of persecutions and the afflictions that we are enduring.
People: To this end we have gathered to worship and to pray, asking God to make us worthy of the call of Jesus on our lives. We will fulfill our call by every good resolve and work of faith so that the name of our Lord Jesus might be glorified.

Call to Confession

Destruction and violence are before us. Strife and contention arise within us. The laws of God become slack and justice does not prevail. The wicked surround us and judgment is perverted. We get weary in doing well. We sin. When we sin, we nail the Blessed Savior in the side again! Let our prayers of confession arise before the throne of God.

Confession

God, we are the wrongdoers who cause trouble. We are the ones filled with violence and self-righteousness. We are the ones who try to make it on our own. Forgive our sin. Help us to worship with holy living, we pray in the Savior's name.

Words of Assurance

Our God is righteous and every judgment is right. Our God is faithful to keep every promise made. Our God loves us. This will never change. This is good news.

Responsive Reading

Leader: We serve the Do Right One.
People: The God we serve is too wise to make mistakes.
Leader: We serve the On Time God.
People: The God we trust is never late or early, but always on time to deliver.
Leader: We serve the Kick Tail, Take No Name God.
People: Those who try to hem us in and take us out ignore God.
Leader: We serve the Never Sleep or Slumber God.
People: Even the small, the young, and the insignificant are protected by God's love.
Leader: We serve the Self-Revealing God.
People: Whatever we need God to become, the I Am is more than able.
Leader: We serve the Trouble Don't Last Always God.
People: The commandments of God are sure and provided the ancestors with what is known as "mother wit" to give us understanding in all areas of life. We might be short in stature among the leaders of this world, but we serve the Omnipotent and Tall God who reigns over all.

Offertory Invitation

Zacchaeus stole from his own people for the sake of earthly wealth. It didn't mean that he didn't want to see Jesus. It meant that he had his priorities mixed up. When he finally saw Jesus, he promised to pay back what he had stolen. To ensure that we don't get caught up like him, let's be generous, for we have seen the Christ.

Offertory Praise

God, we have always been a sharing people. It is in our nature to bless others in the community. Now we give to the wider community. We ask that you would receive these gifts, that the love you have shared with us will spread far and wide. We pray in the name of the Ultimate Giver.

Benediction

Leader: Hurry and let's go to brunch, to the malls, and to our homes. For Jesus wants to stay with us today!

People: Salvation has come to our house. Our temples are ready to host the Lord.

Leader: Go! Write the vision; make it plain on tablets, so that a runner may read it. For there is still a vision for the appointed time; it speaks of the end and does not lie. If it seems to tarry, wait for it; it will surely come, it will not delay.

People: God the Righteous, Jesus Christ the Redeemer, and the Holy Spirit are in us, with us, and waiting on our arrival wherever we go. Hallelujah and amen.

ALL SAINTS DAY

Daniel 7:1–3, 15–18
Psalm 149
Ephesians 1:11–23
Luke 6:20–31

Call to Worship

Leader: Blessed, praised and glorified, exalted, extolled, honored, adored, and lauded be the name of the Holy One, our God.

People: Blessed is God beyond all blessings, hymns, anthems, and songs that are uttered in the world.

Leader: The Creator made the heavens and the earth, the sun, the moon, and the stars.

People: Blessed is the name of our God.

Leader: The world and all that is in it belong to the Holy One.

People: Blessed is the name of our God.

Leader: The Lord of Life gave breath to lumps of clay and made them a little lower than the angels.

People: Magnified and sanctified is the great Name Above All Names, whose mercies we receive.

Leader: The Lord giveth and the Lord taketh away the breath given unto lumps of clay.

People: We bless the Beginning and the End for the memories we have of those who have left us to return unto God. We gather today to re-member the saints who are now with God. And we are reminded that if we want to be prepared to join them we must offer appropriate worship. May the great name of God be blessed forever and ever.

Call to Confession

The God of dreamers, visionaries, great winds, and troubled spirits continues to call us into closer relationship. The days before us are shorter than they were. The signs of the times alert us that eternity is closer than we like to think. We want to be ready when the trumpet sounds. Let us confess.

Confession

God, we are waiting for the time when you will swallow up death forever and wipe away the tears from our eyes. That time is not yet! We want to be like Job and say that it is alright that you have called our loved ones home. But we miss our loved ones and our grief is real. We would like to bless your name, but we often doubt your goodness. We have sinned this past week. Forgive us. Give us new life, we pray, in the name of him who rose again!

Words of Assurance

Hear the good news! The holy ones of the Most High shall receive God's realm and possess it forever—forever and forever. This is the Word of God.
People: Thanks be to God.

Responsive Reading

Leader: It's time for us to offer up high praise unto God.
People: High praise is the sort that blesses God in good times and in bad.
Leader: Both life and death are in the hands of God.
People: The death of a saint is precious in the sight of God.
Leader: Those who have made their calling and election sure, and have been called from life and its mortality to immortality, stand now around the throne.
People: They have joined the angelic choir. They have received new bodies.
Leader: The old has passed away for them. Behold, they don't want to return to this valley of tears.
People: There are no more good-byes there, and every day is sunny and fair.
Leader: They have no worries or concerns. Pains have been wiped away.
People: And there is a tree in the midst of the city of God with leaves good for healing.
Leader: The streets there are paved with gold.
People: All debts have been canceled, and money doesn't matter!
Leader: The Church Triumphant is in session today.
People: The saints are at home! Their living was not in vain. This is the glorious experience for which we are living daily. They are not dead.

They are not even gone away. Today, they live inside of us. Nothing of God's is ever wasted. They touched our lives and await our arrival on the other side. Blessed be the name of our God.

Offertory Invitation

In Christ we have also obtained an inheritance, having been destined according to the purpose of God, who accomplished all things according to the divine purpose and will, so that we have set our hopes on Christ and now live for the praise of his glory. Our giving brings glory to his name. Let us share generously.

Offertory Praise

God, we have just a foretaste of the riches of our glorious inheritance among the saints, and what is the immeasurable greatness of your power for us who believe, according to the working of your Holy Spirit in us. We thank you that the Holy Spirit has prompted us to share in this offering so that the Body of Christ might continue to harvest saints for the eternal realm. We pray in the name of the Head of the Church.

Benediction

Leader: Now, sisters and brothers, I say to us all, "Love your enemies. Do good to those who hate you."
People: We will bless those who curse us and pray for those who abuse us.
Leader: If anyone strikes you on one cheek, offer them the other.
People: If anyone is in need of our coat, we won't hold onto our shirt or blouse.
Leader: Give to everyone who begs from you; and if anyone takes away your goods, do not ask for them again.
People: These are hard sayings. Yet, we want to be numbered in the saints. So, we will do unto others as we would have them do unto us.
Leader: God, the life giver, Jesus Christ, our life ransom, and the Holy Spirit, the life transformer, are already at work in us, on us, for us, and even in spite of us. Go forward in peace and power.
People: We go forth into the world, with death-defying victory in the name of the Glory, the Resurrection, and the Matchless Power. Hallelujah and amen.

PROPER 27 · SUNDAY BETWEEN NOVEMBER 6 AND NOVEMBER 12

Haggai 1:5b–2:9 or Job 19:23–27a
Psalm 145:1–5, 17–21 or Psalm 17:1–9
2 Thessalonians 2:1–5, 13–17
Luke 20:27–38

Call to Worship

Leader: Come, all who are without comfort and in need of blessed consolation.
People: We are those of the diaspora, spread to the four winds, struggling to overcome.
Leader: Take courage, people of God, for our Sovereign is with us.
People: Spirit of the Living God, fall afresh on us.
Leader: Have no fears, ye of little faith. God's Spirit has been with us since the creation.
People: We remember the legends of our reign in Africa with all of its glory.
Leader: God's promise is that the glory is not gone. We are the promised ones.
People: We come to offer our treasure chests to be filled with splendor so that we might give glory to God in worship and praise. Spirit of the Living God, fall afresh on us.

Call to Confession

We must always give thanks to God, brothers and sisters beloved, because God chose us as the first fruits for salvation through sanctification by the Spirit and through belief in the truth. For this purpose we have been called through the proclamation of the good news, so that we might obtain the glory of our Lord Jesus Christ. For the multiple ways that we have hidden the glory in the past week, we have this period of confession. Let us pray.

Confession

God, the lawless one is revealed as Satan. This enemy of ours is destined for destruction. The devil opposes and exalts himself above every so-called god or object of worship, so that he takes his seat in the temple of God, declaring himself to be God. We have fallen into his traps this past week. We have agreed with him and sinned. Forgive us. Wash us. Cleanse us, we pray, in the name of the Beloved Lamb of our Salvation.

Words of Assurance

We are a remnant, scattered to the four corners of the earth. Yet God has called us to work the work of the One who has called us. The promise of God is that in just a little while, the heavens, the earth, the sea, and the nations will be shaken and we shall all be reunited as one people of the Most High. This is our good news.

Responsive Reading

Leader: How excellent is the name of God!
People: We will lift our voices in exaltation all the days of our lives.
Leader: Each dawning of a brand new day calls for my personal adoration for the Creator of time.
People: The majesty of God's created order is greater than any mere words can describe!
Leader: The exploits of the Most High have been preserved and passed down from generation to generation.
People: When we think of God's goodness and mercy, we just can't help giving praise.
Leader: Justice is another name for God, who is gentle towards the whole earth.
People: To all who place their trust in God, just a whisper of the name will connect them.
Leader: God pays attention to our pleas for help. God stores each of our tears.
People: God sends deliverance for the traps set for us. The roving eyes of God are constantly upon us. And the wicked will earn eternal damnation.
Leader: Nothing but praise for the love of God will ever cross my lips.
People: This piece of bitter earth gives glory to God forever and ever.

Offertory Invitation

Jesus is Lord to the glory of God. Jesus is not the God of the dead, but of the living. For to him all people are alive, those who profess the wonderful name as well as those who don't. In order to give nonbelievers another opportunity to hear the story of good news, let us give with thankful hearts.

Offertory Praise

God, the silver is yours. The gold is yours. You are the God of all, of those scattered from one end of the globe to the other. And, by your love for us, we love all whom you love. Receive these, our gifts, in the name of the Greatest Gift.

Benediction

Leader: Now then, my brothers and my sisters, stand firm this week and hold fast to the traditions that we have been taught that bring salvation and liberty. And now may our Lord Jesus Christ and God, the Everlasting Arm, who loved us and through grace gave us eternal comfort and good hope, comfort our hearts and strengthen them in every good work and word in the days ahead.

People: Hallelujah and amen.

PROPER 28 · SUNDAY BETWEEN NOVEMBER 13 AND NOVEMBER 19

Isaiah 65:17–25 or Malachi 4:1–2a
Isaiah 12 or Psalm 98
2 Thessalonians 3:6–13
Luke 21:5–19

Call to Worship

Leader: God is about to create new heavens and a new earth.
People: The former things shall not be remembered or come to mind.
Leader: But we will be glad and rejoice forever in what God is creating.
People: Jerusalem will be God's joy. And we, the inhabitants, will be God's delight.
Leader: We will rejoice in the New Jerusalem and we will be God's great joy.
People: There shall be no more the sound of weeping or our cries of distress.
Leader: No more will an infant live but a few days or an older person not live out a lifetime.
People: The wolf and the lamb shall feed together and, while we are yet speaking, God will hear.
We have come to practice for that great day with sounds of worship and thanksgiving.

Call to Confession

We live in houses that we did not build. We reap the rich harvest of foods that we did not grow. All that we have comes from God, and yet this past week has found us dwelling in themes of discontentment. This is our time for confession.

Confession

God, you have commanded that we keep away from those who live in idleness and walk in paths not consistent with your Word. You have told us to allow others to imitate our lives. We have done what you told us not to do. And we have failed to do what we know we ought to do. We are sinners. We stand in need of your grace. Work in us so that we will not grow weary in doing what is right. We pray in the name of our Righteousness.

Words of Assurance

Shout aloud and sing for joy, O royal Zion, for great in our midst is the Holy One of Israel. This is good news.

Responsive Reading

Leader: We owe God great thanks for being so lenient with us.
People: Our lives have been so ragged that we have earned God's righteous anger.
Leader: Yet God's anger was prevented by God's love, and we, the rebellious, have been mightily comforted.
People: Surely God is my salvation. I will trust and will not be afraid. The Lord is my strength and my power. God is my unfailing hope.
Leader: With joy we draw water from the wells of salvation.
People: This water is thirst quenching and life changing. This water satisfies.
Leader: We owe God big-time thanks.
People: We will make known to the nations all that God has done.
Leader: People of God, let's raise the roof!
People: Our God is an awesome God!

Offertory Invitation

Like the days of a great tree shall the days of God's people be. The chosen of God shall long enjoy the work of their hands. They shall not labor in vain, promises the Almighty. In order that we might live to see the increase of our labors, let us give as unto the God of the Harvest.

Offertory Praise

God, with toil and labor we have lived our whole lives. Not many of us have been born to wealth. Not many of us know what the silver spoon looks like. But you have blessed us to know the power of cocreating with you. Receive these gifts from our hands, in the name of the One Who Is Coming.

Benediction

Leader: Go into the world! And when you hear of wars and insurrections, do not be terrified, for these things must take place first, but the end will not follow immediately.

People: We leave considering how nation rises against nation and kingdom against kingdom; there are great earthquakes and in various places famines and plagues; and there are dreadful and great signs from heaven.

Leader: God the Mind, Jesus the Head of the Body, and the Holy Spirit, the Power, keep us faithful until the end!

People: Hallelujah and amen.

PROPER 29 · THE REIGN OF CHRIST
SUNDAY BETWEEN NOVEMBER 20 AND NOVEMBER 26

Jeremiah 23:1–6
Luke 1:68–79 or Psalm 46
Colossians 1:11–20
Luke 23:33–43

Call to Worship

Leader: All hail the power of Jesus' strong name!
People: Christ is King to the glory of God.
Leader: With the angels let us worship the Worthy Lamb.
People: We come to cast every care at Jesus' feet and receive relief from the burdens of our lives.
Leader: Christ is King!
People: To God be glory!

Call to Confession

Jesus Christ, the Good Shepherd, has shown us how sheep are tenderly cared for in good times and in bad. Jesus laid down his life for us when he could have called the angelic host for deliverance. We have taken up his cross. And, in this past week, we have made the Shepherd of Our Soul look bad. Thank God for a period of confession.

Confession

God, your love for us is so amazing. We continue to struggle with the fact that the King of Glory dared to come to step on the down elevator of heaven, put on human skin, and move into our contemporary communities. It yet stuns our mind to realize that Jesus gave up his divinity so that we might share it. We have sinned. We ask for your forgiveness. We ask for restoration that we might be good shepherds to others, leading them into your fold. We pray in the name of Christ, the King.

Words of Assurance

God has gathered us as a remnant of the flock out of all the lands where we have been driven. God has made us fruitful and given us the ability to multiply and to reproduce. God has given us shepherds who watch over our souls. The Righteous Branch is our Savior who will reign as King, dealing wisely, executing justice and righteousness in the land. This is good news.

Responsive Reading

Leader: Blessed be the Lord, who came to set every captive free.
People: The power of salvation is the center of our joy.
Leader: From the house of David, the throne of God was prophesied through the holy prophets.
People: David, the little shepherd boy, won deliverance from the enemies for God.
Leader: God's mercy and kindness was sworn to Abram and Sarai by covenant.
People: The Good Shepherd came through David's seed to rescue us from fear so that we might live in holiness and righteousness all the days of our lives.
Leader: Jesus, the Most High, descended to prepare the way to glory for us.
People: He was the perfect role model and example to show us God with human flesh.
Leader: The blood of Jesus cleanses us from our sin and covers us in the righteousness of God.
People: We have forgiveness of our sin, by the blood.
Leader: By the tender mercies of God, the dawning from on high has broken upon us.
People: We can see clearly now; the gloom and stench of death is gone. The King has come.
The King reigns within us. The King will come again soon. And we shall experience world peace! Reign, Jesus, reign!

Offertory Invitation

Jesus Christ, the King of Glory, is coming with the clouds; every eye will see him, even those who crucified him. The saints will be enraptured to meet the thief who cried, "Remember me." To ensure that all who want to be can be ready, let us prepare our hearts to give.

Offertory Praise

God, your realm is not of this world. You have a realm not prepared by human hands. We want to inhabit it throughout eternity. We have given these gifts in your name and for your glory. May they help your realm to come as we pray in the name of the Soon Coming King.

Benediction

Leader: May we be made strong with all the strength that comes from the glorious power of Christ the King.

People: We leave prepared to endure everything that comes our way with patience, while joyfully giving thanks unto God, who has enabled us to share in the inheritance of the saints in the Light.

Leader: Go into the world testifying that we have been rescued from the power of evil and transferred into the community of the Beloved Son, in whom we have redemption and the forgiveness of sin.

People: Jesus Christ, the Ruler, is before all things, and in him all things hold together. He is the head of the Body, the Church; he is the beginning, the firstborn from the dead, so that he might come to have first place in everything.

Leader: In Jesus, all the fullness of God was pleased to dwell, and through Jesus God was pleased to reconcile to God's own self all things, whether on earth or in heaven, by making peace through the blood of the cross. Go, in the shalom of God. God, the King Sender; Christ, the Ruler; and the Holy Spirit, the Ruler's Announcer, enfold us until we meet again.

People: Hallelujah and amen.

7 · ADDITIONAL SERVICE

BAPTISM OF AN ADULT

Organ Prelude

Introit

"Trust and Obey" (*African-American Heritage Hymnal* [Chicago: GIA Publications], 380)

Call to Worship

Leader: Christ loved the Church and gave himself up for it, that he might sanctify it, having cleansed it by the washing of the water with the Word, that he might present to himself a glorious Church, not having spot or wrinkle or any such thing. But the Church is to be holy and without blemish.

People: Wherefore, as a beloved community, let us be steadfast, unmovable, always abounding in the work of the Lord, as we know that our labor is not in vain. Our faith is not in vain. And our baptism is not in vain. We give thanks for the baptism, a sign of our new life in Jesus Christ.

Hymn

"Wash, Oh God, Our Sons and Daughters" (*African-American Heritage Hymnal*, 674)

Invocation

Call to Confession

Leader: Baptism is both God's gift and our human response to this gift. Our baptism only points us toward our growth into the measure of the maturity of the whole Body of Christ. As we gather, we acknowledge the necessity of faith for the reception of the salvation embodied and set forth in baptism as evidenced by Jesus and as a command to the Church. Baptism is not simply a momentary experience of those being baptized, but a reminder of the vows we made when we went willingly into the cooling waters. This is our time to confess the sin that separates us from God and nullifies our baptismal vows. Let us pray.

Confession

God, we get to be reminded of all that our baptism means as we gather to baptize an adult. This is so different from that of an infant or a youth. This is one who has had life experiences that could have led to death and destruction. This is one who has made a conscious choice to become a follower of your way, your will, and your wisdom. This is one who is ready to follow in our footsteps. And we know who we are today! Forgive our sin. Cleanse us from our unrighteousness. Restore us to you as you remove our sin as far as the east is from the west. Help us to be the ones that this new believer can follow and imitate. We pray in the name of Jesus Christ.

Words of Assurance

Baptism is not just a momentary experience, but a lifelong growth into Christ. As baptized believers we are called to reflect the glory of God as we are transformed by the power of the Holy Spirit into the likeness of Christ. It is God who gives us both the will and the ability to be changed. This is good news.

The Word of God: Matthew 3:13–17

Leader: Jesus came from Galilee to John at the Jordan River to be baptized.
People: John did not want to baptize Jesus because he recognized his divinity.
Leader: John told Jesus, "I am the one who needs to be baptized by you. Why do you come to me?"
People: The response of Jesus was, "Let it happen this way now. For this is the proper sequence to fulfill the plan of God."

Leader: Then John baptized Jesus in the waters before witnesses.

People: When Jesus came up from the water, suddenly the heavens were opened to him. Jesus saw the Spirit of God descending like a dove and alighting upon him. And the voice of God thundered from heaven, "This is my Son, the Beloved, with whom I am well pleased."

Leader: Baptism was a full family event.

People: Baptism remains a full family event. We are family. We share in this awe-filled and inspiring occasion as we welcome into this family a new member because of his/her confession of our common faith.

Leader: Baptism reminds us, refreshes us, and renews in us our collective memory of participation in Christ's death, burial, and resurrection.

People: Our conversion, our pardon, and our cleansing by the Holy Spirit through the washing of the water and the Living Word incorporate us into the Body of Christ.

Leader: Baptism is our initial step into the reign of God. It is our formal and public acknowledgment of our new life in Christ.

People: Baptism is a rich, sacred, and holy symbol of our Christian faith. Baptism is the ritual of our personal outward confession of an inward commitment to God. We remember our baptism and we are grateful. Thanks be unto God.

Confession of our Faith

Leader: Jesus Christ, the head of the Church, has given us a solid command and authority to take these to the waters. What is our charge?

People: We are disciples of Jesus Christ, who told us to go into all the world and to teach all nations. We are to baptize them into the name of God the Creator, God the Redeemer, and God the Holy Spirit. Jesus declared that whosoever believe in their hearts, confess with their mouths, and are baptized shall be saved. This candidate has met the conditions of induction into the Body of Christ.

Hymn

"Where He Leads Me" (*African-American Heritage Hymnal,* 550)

Prayer of Presentation

Our gracious and merciful God, we present this your servant _____ , who, believing upon Jesus Christ, your Son and our Savior, and repenting and renouncing all sin, would obey in all that you have commanded. As this one now agrees to follow Christ into the watery grave of baptism, may she/he indeed put on Christ and rise with Christ to walk in newness of life. Clothe this one, we pray, with the whole armor of God: the breast-plate of righteousness, the shield of faith, the helmet of salvation, and the sword of the Spirit; so that this new believer might be girdled about with truth, feet shod with the preparation of the gospel of peace, able to with-stand in the evil day and, having done all, stand. Mightily work within this one by your light and power that he/she may be preserved from all error and maintained in the patience, perseverance, and victory of the saints of the ages. Let this person's name not be blotted out of the Lamb's Book of Life, but let this believer have a place with those of every nation who, coming out of great tribulation, have washed their robes and made them white in the blood of the Lamb. Receive this one, we pray, in the name of the Christ.

Baptism

"Take Me to the Water" (*African-American Heritage Hymnal,* 675)

Charge to the Newly Baptized

Leader: Beloved, you have publicly professed your faith and received the blessed seal of that covenant, whereby you are now dedicated to Christ. You have all the benefits of his redemption forever. It is incumbent upon you that you give all diligence to make your calling and election sure, adding to your faith, virtue; and to virtue, knowledge; and to knowledge, temperance; and to temperance, patience; and to patience, godliness; and to godliness, kindness; and to kindness, love. For if these things be in you and abound, they will make you so that you will never be barren or un-fruitful in the knowledge of our Lord. Your baptism has ushered you into the abundant reign of our Lord and Savior, Jesus Christ.

People: We welcome you into the community of faith and, even greater, into the Church Universal. We covenant to be faithful to you and with you in constantly reaffirming this baptismal vow.

Leader: What shall we now say, to this our brother/sister? Shall we con-tinue in sin, that grace may abound?

People: God forbid! How shall we, that are dead to sin, live any longer therein? We know that as many of us as were baptized into Jesus Christ were baptized into his death. Therefore, we are buried with him by bap-tism unto death, that, as Christ was raised up from the dead by the glory and power of God, even so, we also should walk in newness of life. We walk together in Christian love.

Song of Benediction

"He Looked Beyond My Faults!" (*African-American Heritage Hymnal,* 249)

Other books from The Pilgrim Press

TRUMPET IN ZION
Worship Resources, Year A

LINDA H. HOLLIES

ISBN 0-8298-1410-8/paper/214 pages/$14.00

Trumpet in Zion, Year A addresses God in the voice, verbiage, and expression of African Americans in worship. Based on the *Revised Common Lectionary,* this resource offers clergy, worship planners, and lay leaders the opportunity to utilize the Bible in new and engaging ways with their congregations.

TRUMPET IN ZION
Worship Resources, Year B

LINDA H. HOLLIES

ISBN 0-8298-1477-9/paper/214 pages/$14.00

Following the structure of the *Revised Common Lectionary,* this resource includes calls to worship, prayers of confession, words of assurance, responsive readings, offertory invitations, and blessings for each Sunday. It is also highly adaptable, making it an ideal resource for congregations who do not follow the lectionary.

To order these or any other books from The Pilgrim Press, call or write to:

THE PILGRIM PRESS
700 PROSPECT AVENUE EAST
CLEVELAND, OHIO 44115-1100

Phone orders **1-800-537-3394** ▪ *Fax orders* **216-736-2206**

Please include shipping charges of $4.00 for the first book and $0.75 for each additional book. Or order from our web sites at www.pilgrimpress.com and www.ucpress.com.

Prices subject to change without notice.